The media's watching Vault!
Here's a sampling of our coverage.

"For those hoping to climb the ladder of success, [Vault's] insights are priceless."
– *Money magazine*

"The best place on the web to prepare for a job search."
– *Fortune*

"[Vault guides] make for excellent starting points for job hunters and should be purchased by academic libraries for their career sections [and] university career centers."
– *Library Journal*

"The granddaddy of worker sites."
– *U.S. News & World Report*

"A killer app."
– *New York Times*

One of Forbes' 33 "Favorite Sites"
– *Forbes*

"To get the unvarnished scoop, check out Vault."
– *Smart Money Magazine*

"Vault has a wealth of information about major employers and job-searching strategies as well as comments from workers about their experiences at specific companies."
– *The Washington Post*

"A key reference for those who want to know what it takes to get hired by a law firm and what to expect once they get there."
– *New York Law Journal*

"Vault [provides] the skinny on working conditions at all kinds of companies from current and former employees."
– *USA Today*

VAULT
> the most trusted name in career information™

VAULT CAREER GUIDE TO
JOURNALISM & INFORMATION MEDIA

VAULT CAREER GUIDE TO
JOURNALISM & INFORMATION MEDIA

**STEPHEN WARLEY
AND THE STAFF OF VAULT**

For information about permission to reproduce selections from this book, contact Vault Inc., 150 W. 22nd St., 5th Floor, New York, NY 10011, (212) 366-4212.

Library of Congress Cataloging-in-Publication Data

ISBN 1-58131-355-1

Printed in the United States of America

ACKNOWLEDGMENTS

Stephen Warley's acknowledgements: I would like to thank my family and colleagues for their support throughout my career. I would like to extend special thanks to the following people for their help in the development of this book: Karen Beckers, CBS News, Gwen Billings, Cynopsis Kids, Ryan Cline, Magazine Photo Editor/Producer, Dr. Everette Dennis, Fordham University, Don Fitzpatrick, TVSpy.com, Kate Guttman, Sesame Workshop, Judlyne Lilly, Second Street Dreams, Michael Mitchell, The Medicines Company, Daisy Pareja, ParejaMediaMatch, James Sheridan, InterPositive Media, Larry Tsironis, The Rose Group.

Vault's acknowledgments: We are extremely grateful to Vault's entire staff for all their help in the editorial, production and marketing processes. Vault also would like to acknowledge the support of our investors, clients, employees, family, and friends. Thank you!

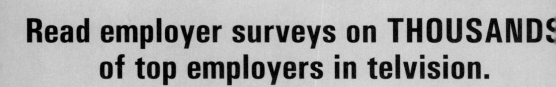

Table of Contents

Visit Vault at www.vault.com for insider company profiles, expert advice,
career message boards, expert resume reviews, the Vault Job Board and more.

VAULT CAREER LIBRARY

ix

Visit Vault at www.vault.com for insider company profiles, expert advice, career message boards, expert resume reviews, the Vault Job Board and more.

VAULT CAREER LIBRARY

xi

Defining Journalism & Information Media

CHAPTER 1

Journalism and Information Media encompasses a wide variety of different media and organizations, creating content that informs, inspires and educates consumers. The media career paths that will be addressed in this book include:

- Newspapers
- Magazines
- Radio News
- Television News
- Documentaries
- Public Relations
- Online Media
- Children's Media
- Ethnic Media

For decades, media content was neatly categorized as either "news" or "entertainment." In the past 20 years, media has mushroomed into one of the largest sectors of the American economy. New magazine titles, radio formats, cable channels and web sites have proliferated, blurring the lines between news and entertainment.

With the Information Age now in full swing, the term "news" no longer fully represents the thousands of media outlets that now provide consumers with information as a resource to enrich their lives beyond delivering the headlines of the day. For example, the ultimate goal of children's media is to help educate children, but it uses entertainment as the vehicle to deliver its message.

The domain of newsgathering is no longer exclusive to newspapers, radio, magazines and television. Public relations has come to play a vital role in the gathering and distribution of information. However, it is "platform neutral," owning no means of direct distribution. To better reflect the various forms of media that now inform us, the term "information media" as been included in the title of this guide.

Visit Vault at www.vault.com for insider company profiles, expert advice, career message boards, expert resume reviews, the Vault Job Board and more.

VAULT CAREER LIBRARY

1

Why Pursue a Career In Journalism & Information Media?

If you are a highly independent and creative person seeking a career in which every day is different, journalism and information media may be the path for you! The very nature of newsgathering puts you in contact with an array of interesting people, and you are always presented with the opportunity to learn new ideas.

You will get to share these exciting on-the-job experiences not only with your family and friends, but also with your local community, all of America and the world. For better or for worse, the information you help to gather and distribute impacts the lives of millions of people. In some cases, there can be quite a bit of travel involved in covering stories on the road, especially as you gain experience and climb the proverbial corporate ladder.

While journalism and information media offers an exciting career path, there are some downsides. In most media sectors, the pay is very low to start, but over time there are opportunities for financial success. It's a basic supply and demand issue. There are always more people trying to get into media than there are jobs being created.

Every day may be different, but that means the hours are also likely to be very irregular, making your schedule hellish at times. All-nighters are not uncommon, no matter which medium you work in. Most work environments are deadline driven. In today's world, maintaining budgets are always a concern as well. Tight deadlines and budgets will force you to deal with a healthy amount of pressure.

What Executives & Managers Want Now

In a recent study analyzing the digital media strategies of the top 25 media companies by Fordham Business School, top executives across broadcast, print and online indicated they increasingly sought media professionals who were more entrepreneurial and possessed a broader understanding of a variety of disciplines, rather than a specialized focus. Some of the traits and skills they described included creativity, flexibility, understanding of technology and basic business knowledge.

Most of the executives agreed that a "super-media professional," a person who could perform all the basic functions of a media operation, still needs additional intangibles to thrive in the digital media world. Many believe there will continue to be a clear division of labor between the technology, content and business areas. However, there will now be greater bridges of understanding between the various disciplines. For example, a producer will continue to create content, but will now require a greater understanding of technology and business to better perform their job. This evolution in workflow will also help to promote greater teamwork. The illustration below captures the blending knowledge base of each of the primary disciplines in media.

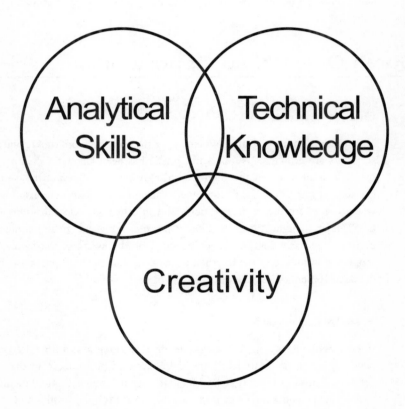

Visit Vault at **www.vault.com** for insider company profiles, expert advice,
career message boards, expert resume reviews, the Vault Job Board and more.

VAULT CAREER LIBRARY   3

For those just launching their career in media, managers want to see hands-on experience, in addition to a journalism degree. Understanding how to use a software program, like Final Cut Pro, shooting with a digital video camera, using HTML and exploiting the Internet as a research tool are also highly attractive skills to managers. Business knowledge, such as knowing how to develop a basic budget or a marketing plan, will also give you an edge on the competition.

Many media organizations operate under tight budgets and don't offer training and development programs as other industries do, so it is important to bring some experience to the table. Many newspapers, radio stations, television stations, magazines and web sites have internship programs and welcome the help. Not only is this a great way to gain experience, but it will help you begin building a network of contacts when you start searching for your first job.

Some Overlooked Opportunities

Online media

New Internet companies are now emerging from the dot-com rubble and the survivors are growing. No aspect of media has been left untouched by the indelible impression of the Internet. Simply put, the Internet has shifted greater and greater control to consumers, changing their expectations of how, when and where they consume news and information. Organizations like CBS News, Knight-Ridder or *Time Magazine* represent great journalistic traditions and seemingly offer job security, but be aware of the increasing scope and influence of the Internet; to overlook this medium poses a risk to the development of your career.

Freelance work

It goes without saying that everyone would prefer a full-time job with benefits, but those "staff jobs" are highly coveted positions in media. To break into the industry or if you are looking to switch into a different medium, you should consider freelance positions. Some are full time without benefits and others may lead to a staff job. Looking for a job on the inside as a freelancer sure beats knocking on doors from the outside!

Smaller companies

Generally, smaller organizations offer the opportunity for more responsibility than would a larger organization. Small radio stations, television stations or newspapers offer recent college graduates the opportunity to gain more experience more quickly, helping them stand out from the crowd when they search for their second job.

Keep working, even without pay

Between your internship and your first job, don't stay idle. Keep developing your skills, even if it's not within the structure of a company. Web sites, blogs, moblogs, digital video cameras and lap-top editing systems enable you to create content, as well as publish it for consumption by a world-wide audience on the Internet. Having your own blog, web site or digital videos demonstrates your initiative. Who knows, if it's good enough, maybe you will be offered a position beyond the entry level.

Game Plan for Getting Hired

Your needs, your personal brand

If you don't know "who you are" or what you want to do, most hiring managers will overlook you. They want to hire someone who is passionate about the job they are trying to fill, and they'll sense whether or not you are sincere about your intentions.

Most people erroneously believe that the wider the range of jobs they are willing to apply for, the greater their chances for getting hired. The exact opposite is true. The more focused you are about what you want to do, the more opportunities will come your way. You need to develop a "personal brand," so people clearly understand what your strengths are and the type of job you want. As you network, people will come to associate you with your distinct attributes. As they hear of job openings, they will match you up with jobs that are appropriate for your skills and desires.

Be clear about your general career path, whether you want to be a producer or a writer or if you want to work in sales or marketing. If you want to be a producer in television, but are having a tough time landing a job, try producing for radio, so you can begin to build your producing skills. Be true to yourself. Don't tell a hiring manger what you think they want to hear.

Visit Vault at www.vault.com for insider company profiles, expert advice, career message boards, expert resume reviews, the Vault Job Board and more.

VAULT CAREER LIBRARY

5

Networking

Most people in media find work through networking. As soon as you know what you want to do, start reaching out to people who work in the industry to build your contacts. Ask your friends, your relatives, your parents' friends, your professors, colleagues at your internship and anyone else you think may be of help. Even if the potential contact is a few degrees removed, it is a closer relationship to build upon than being interviewed by a complete stranger.

As you collect contact names, keep them well organized. Even if they don't lead to interviews in the short term, something may come up over the long term. Stay in touch. Organizing your contact information in a simple Excel spreadsheet will be a huge help in keeping on top of all your contacts. Try to touch base every three months or so.

Contact managers directly

Unless a job posting tells you to send your resume and cover letter to human resources (HR), don't. For all intents and purposes, HR is a black hole in media. Most hiring is conducted by the manager to whom you would be directly reporting at the company. The media business is driven by personalities, so most managers want to conduct the interview process themselves to see if they can work with a potential new employee or not.

Resume & cover letter

Here are some suggestions for ways to tailor your resume when applying for jobs in news and information media:

- Highlight special projects you have worked on or led. Don't list general duties alone. Include details about the scope of the project and how large an audience it reached.

- If you are applying for sales or marketing positions, be sure to quantify your successes. Share how much revenue you helped develop or how much you increased interest in the service you marketed at a summer job or internship.

- Don't over-embellish your accomplishments; it's a relatively small industry, so the truth is bound to come out.

As for your cover letter, think of it as a written statement of your "personal brand." Tell your prospective employer about the unique skills you have to bring to the table and how this position fits in with your career goals.

It is also important to remember to address each of the skills or traits listed in the job description in your cover letter. Show how your experiences fulfill each of these desired requirements. For example, if the job description states, "Seeking an entrepreneurial individual with a nose for news and exceptional organizational skills for an opening as an associate producer," then draw on your experiences to show how you are entrepreneurial, have strong news judgment and are well organized. End your note with a definitive time as to when you will follow up, unless the job posting specifically states no phone calls.

Creative samples

Unlike most other careers, your resume and cover letter aren't always enough to land a job in a creative field like media. Most positions focused on writing like producing, public relations or reporting will require writing samples. In the case of television or radio news, a demo tape is required for those interested in on-air positions. Some organizations will also conduct writing tests. As you begin your job search, double check to see if additional materials will be requested as part of the hiring process.

Interview process

There is no standard interview process within journalism and information media. It varies from sector to sector and from organization to organization. Even if you are applying for a job in a creative environment, always dress in business attire. Just because everyone in the company is dressed casually doesn't mean you can. You aren't an employee yet, so put your best foot forward.

Don't be fazed by strange questions; just answer to the best of your ability. Study up on the company, so it will be clear that you are interested in them. Try to reinforce the points you made in your cover letter as to why you are qualified for the job. Also, don't be afraid to ask questions about the job and company. You are checking them out, just as much as they are checking out you. Just don't ask about money or salary. Put those questions off until they have offered you a job.

Follow-through notes

The most overlooked and probably the most important document in your job search process is the follow-through note, more commonly known as the

Visit Vault at **www.vault.com** for insider company profiles, expert advice, career message boards, expert resume reviews, the Vault Job Board and more.

VAULT CAREER LIBRARY

7

thank you note. Even if you don't want the job, it's polite to send a thank you note. You don't want to burn any bridges. Right after you leave your interview, you should sit down and write your thank you while your interview is still fresh in your head.

In addition to offering your thanks, point out something in the interview that confirms why you want the job. If one of your shortcomings was brought out in the interview, state how you would resolve it if you were hired. Try to personalize the note. If there was a particular industry issue you discussed in the interview, offer up some follow up information if it is appropriate. To be on the safe side, both e-mail and mail your note.

Tips for Managing Your Career

The goal of your first job is to land your second job

Your first job is hardly the biggest decision you will ever make in your life, but it will have enormous influence over the future course of your career. Once you land your first job you are finally in "the club." Your first priority is to master all the duties you have been hired to do and to find ways to accomplish them more efficiently, so you can take on more responsibility. After a few months you should be thinking about your next step and setting goals for yourself to gather the necessary experience that will make you qualified for your second job.

Mentors

While the only person who will ever care about the growth of your career is you, seek out a mentor to help you develop your career. Approach someone you think you can trust, who is willing to show you the ropes. This person may become a valuable recommendation when you are searching for your second job. He/she can also help you sidestep some career landmines along the way.

Moving around is no longer taboo

Unlike your parents, you most likely will never have the opportunity to work for the same company for 10, 20 or 30 years. When you feel you have stopped gaining new knowledge and experiences, it's time to move on. It is not uncommon for media professionals to move around a lot during the early phase of their careers. Staying at the same company may offer stability, but also creates stagnation in your career. Changing jobs every couple of years means more money, more responsibility, more personal contacts and more respect.

Keep your career moving forward

Inevitably almost every media professional is faced with a period in their career in which they feel stuck, or fear they have lost sight of their career goals. In a highly competitive, creative and high-pressure industry like media, this is perfectly normal.

The key to developing your career and to maintaining your happiness is to be always gaining new experiences and constantly challenging yourself. Resting on your laurels or coasting is not an option. It is important to remember to maintain the consistency of the essence of your career and not to become fixated on a particular title or company. For example, if the essence of your career is to produce content and you have spent much of your career in television, you may consider producing content in public relations or for the Internet. These are new environments that will offer you new challenges and maybe even more money, while staying true to the core of your career – producing content.

Special Education & Training

Journalism degrees

For some, going back to school for a graduate degree is another option to get their career moving forward again. Undergraduate degrees in journalism and communications aren't required for most positions in media, but they certainly don't hurt. Many media professionals have varying backgrounds with strong communication skills. For example, someone who worked on Wall Street as an analyst may leverage their business skills and contacts to become a business reporter for radio or a magazine. Graduate degrees in journalism also give people from other fields the basic knowledge to make the switch into careers in news and information media.

Visit Vault at **www.vault.com** for insider company profiles, expert advice, career message boards, expert resume reviews, the Vault Job Board and more.

V/\ULT CAREER LIBRARY   9

Pursuing an MBA

In recent years, more and more media professionals have become interested in pursuing their Masters of Business Administration (MBA), particularly those on the business side. Schools like NYU, Fordham and UCLA have special concentrations in media as part of their MBA programs. Only those seriously considering a business path in media should pursue their MBA. It provides a solid foundation of business skills, but having an MBA is still not an automatic ticket to the managerial level. As new media technologies continue to be exploited and direct marketing gains influence over the media landscape, the MBA degree may become more important.

Acquiring technical knowledge

Working with new technologies has become a standard component of every media professional's career. Depending on your track, find out what computer programs or technologies will be beneficial for you to learn. If you are interested in marketing, Excel will be a critical tool for you to learn. If you are interested in television production, it is suggested that you learn how to shoot your own video with a digital video camera and how to edit on a laptop editing system, like Final Cut Pro. Enhancing your technical skills will definitely give you an edge over someone who only spent their summer internship getting coffee for Katie Couric.

Newspapers

Newspapers were the first great mass medium, uniting local communities in ways they had never been before. Benjamin Franklin was one of the first newspaper moguls in America. He shrewdly controlled both the production and distribution of his newspaper, *The Pennsylvania Gazette*. He was a printer, and wrote many of the articles himself under various pen names. He also served as postmaster, overseeing the delivery of his own newspaper. By the time of the American Revolution, there were 37 newspapers with a combined weekly circulation of just 5,000 copies in the 13 colonies.

Newspapers would give birth to other great titans like William Randolph Hearst, whose "yellow journalism" was believed to have helped ignite the Spanish-American War; Joseph Pulitzer, journalist and publisher for whom the most coveted prize in journalism is named; Adolph Ochs, publisher of *The New York Times*, who coined the phrase, "All the News That's Fit to Print;" Katharine Graham, Chairman & CEO of The Washington Post Company, one of the most powerful women the newspaper industry has ever seen.

Newspapers enjoyed their height more than 70 years ago and have been in decline ever since, due to rising production costs, the introduction of electronic mediums, and changing reading habits. They still play a vital role as "watchdogs" in many local communities, as well as providing a "public record" in an increasingly cluttered media landscape.

What makes newspapers unique?

In addition to its mobility and relatively low price, the most voracious readers of newspapers would say it is the serendipity of the newspaper that makes it special above all other media. It's the surprise of coming across a story that you might not otherwise find, let alone read, that makes newspapers a treasure.

Today's web surfers would say the Internet has developed its own version of serendipity, drawing them deeper and deeper into a virtual world, almost as if you needed to leave a trail of cheese to find your way back out. Thankfully, the "mouse" can lead the way!

Visit Vault at www.vault.com for insider company profiles, expert advice, career message boards, expert resume reviews, the Vault Job Board and more.

VAULT CAREER LIBRARY   11

What attracts people to work for a newspaper?

Those who are drawn to newspaper work, whether as a journalist or a sales account executive, relish the idea of serving a local community. Most enjoy the unpredictable nature of the business. Every day is truly different. Many newspaper employees are very independent, goal-driven and enjoy the pressure of meeting deadlines. Newspapers also provide an environment in which you are constantly meeting new people, as well as learning new facts and ideas.

Many journalists are attracted to newspapers because of the opportunity to build strong ties and reliable sources in local communities, something few journalists in other media are able to do. Print journalists also enjoy the challenge of using words alone to connect with the community they serve. They weave together facts, bits of information and quotes to tell a story, all without the aid of video or sound.

Is a Career in Newspapers for You?

Lifestyle

If you desire a career in which every day is different, than working for a newspaper will be right up your alley. Of course, the hours are long and few pursue a career in journalism in hopes of becoming wealthy. Don't worry, you won't starve. Once your career hits its stride, you should make a comfortable living. Entry-level pay is definitely low, but this is the period of your career where you want to focus on gaining experience and honing your journalism skills, or on the business side, your sales skills.

The hours are long and irregular. News doesn't just happen from 9 a.m. to 5 p.m.; the Internet has now made news available on demand to consumers at any time they want. Newspapers have been adjusting to this new phenomenon as the Internet grows in influence. Increasingly, newspapers are becoming sensitive to work/life balance issues; offering part-time work, job sharing and work-at-home options.

Each day can be a roller coaster ride from covering a high profile event to the run-of-the-mill story you felt like you've done a thousand times. There is also enormous satisfaction in having your name in print, and in knowing that you are providing information that can positively impact the lives of the community you are serving.

Desired skills & traits

Tenacity: Whether your motivation is to meet a deadline, to beat the competition or to break a story, persistence in getting the story and its facts straight is crucial to becoming a successful journalist.

Communication Skills: Strong verbal and written talents are at the very heart of newsgathering and reporting. Listening is often an understated skill, but crucial. Once facts have been gathered, reporting involves putting them into perspective to capture all sides of a story.

Attention to Detail: Otherwise overlooked bits of information have compromised numerous journalism careers, as has recently occurred at The New York Times and the BBC. Every bit of information must be scrutinized. Organizational skills are also a must to maintain sources, to meet deadlines and to keep on top of ongoing news situations.

People Skills: Journalists may be regarded as wordsmiths, but their profession can also be viewed as managing networks of relationships. How you relate to your co-workers, the community and your sources will vastly influence the quality of your stories. Empathy and persuasiveness go hand in hand when forging strong professional relationships.

Career Track

Content track

Editorial or Desk Assistant: The entry-level position in the world of newspapers. Duties range from administrative tasks to writing brief articles if the copy desk is overwhelmed. Smaller newspapers are more likely to offer more responsibility than larger newspapers, but have fewer resources. With cutbacks in staff, editorial assistants are playing a more direct role in the newsgathering and reporting process.

Salary range: $20,000 to $30,000

Copyeditor or Proofreader: This position requires meticulous attention to detail. They are primarily responsible for checking spelling, grammar errors and facts. They may also check layouts or proofs. No one likes to have their work picked apart, so don't take anything personally when a reporter gives you some guff. It's your job to make the copy look perfect. Generally, you must pass a copy test to land the job.

Visit Vault at **www.vault.com** for insider company profiles, expert advice, career message boards, expert resume reviews, the Vault Job Board and more.

VAULT CAREER LIBRARY   **13**

Salary range: $10 to $35 per hour

Reporter: The frontline position of newsgathering and reporting on news events. Most of the time is spent chasing down interviews, verifying facts, developing sources and gathering facts and quotes into a cohesive story. Reporters today are also called upon as experts of their beat or the topic area they cover, like business, health or politics. They are interviewed by other journalists in other media like radio, magazines and television.

Salary range: $25,000 to $125,000

Photographer: Photography is largely contracted out to freelancers. Most newspapers also depend on photos from archives like Getty Images or the Associated Press. If you are just starting out, establish a relationship with the local newspapers in your area, as well as signing up with a local recruiting agency.

Graphic Artist: Responsible for development of graphics, illustrations and other non-photo images. Depending on the size of the newspaper, they also oversee the layout and design of each edition.

Salary range: $20,000 to $65,000

Editor: Assigns stories, oversees the layout of the newspaper and ensures the editorial standards of the newspaper are maintained. In a management capacity, they also hire and fire reporters, photographers and graphic artists, as well as oversee the budget.

Today, many editors are also required to keep an eye on the latest market trends and readership surveys. In smaller markets, they may also write some of the copy. At larger papers, an editor-in-chief may oversee several editors responsible for different sections of the newspaper, including national news, local news, international news, sports, business and the arts.

Salary range: $25,000 to $150,000

Business Track

Account Executive: On the business side of newspapers, advertising is the lifeblood of the business, even for newspapers that charge a subscription. The sales force develops sales leads by making cold calls, and then follows up on leads in hopes of closing on a deal. If you are enthusiastic and love the rush of making a sale, this is the career for you.

Salary range: $25,000 to $100,000

Marketing and Promotion: To make advertising sales more robust, newspapers need to make sure the circulation in their target community is as large as possible. Marketers will use direct mail pieces, the newspaper's web site and partnerships with local radio or television to attract subscribers. They will also make sure the newspaper is prominently placed on newsstands and in local stores. Depending on the size of their budget, they will also conduct research about the target community to be used by the editor(s) and sales force to better serve the community and advertisers.

Salary range for entry-level positions: $20,000 to $25,000

Publisher: The top job in newspaper industry outside of the owner. Primary focus is on making sure the newspaper is a profitable venture. The wall between sales and editorial used to be formidable, but increasingly, publishers have become involved with the editorial direction of newspapers, particularly if the venture is in financial trouble.

INSIGHTS FROM INDUSTRY LEADERS

Bryan Monroe

Assistant Vice President, News, Knight Ridder

As Assistant Vice President, News, Monroe helps set the overall news direction for the Knight Ridder organization. He has held the position since 2002. Previously, he served as Deputy Managing Editor of Local News, Visuals and Technology at the *San Jose Mercury News*. He was a Nieman fellow at Harvard University in 2002 and graduated from the University of Washington in 1987.

Knight Ridder is the second-largest newspaper publisher in the U.S. It owns 31 dailies, including the *Detroit Free Press*, *Forth Worth Star-Telegram* and *The Miami Herald*. It also operates more than 100 local news web sites as part of the Real Cities network, and co-founded CareerBuilder and Classified Ventures.

Q: What is the strength of newspapers over all other media?

A: Our strengths come in many forms. We have depth and immediacy, enabling us to go deeper than many other media. We also have the strength of trust; people know that they can turn to us and believe what they're reading. We do all that every day. For 50 cents a day, readers can have us on their doorsteps every morning by 6 a.m.

Q: How is the Internet forcing newspapers to evolve and change?

A: We have to be much more of a 24-hour news operation now. Traditionally, we have focused on our deadlines and newsgathering process to deliver content for our readers the next morning. We go to the press at 11 p.m. at night. Stories have to be in at 9 p.m. to be edited and laid out on a page, which means they have to be written by 6 p.m.

Now that we are publishing on multiple platforms, not just in ink on dead trees, we have to write stories as soon as they happen. As developments occur and we gather more information from the scene, we add that to the story we have published online.

Q: Traditionally, broadcasters and newspapers regarded themselves as complementary. Has the web now made your relationship more competitive?

A: In many cases, we are actually partnering with them. Most of our Knight Ridder papers have partnerships with local television stations. We may have our reporters show up on their nightly newscasts or do inserts throughout the day. On the Web, there are great partnership opportunities. In Tampa, we have one centralized newsroom that serves print, online and television. They all draw upon the same content.

Q: What recommendations can you offer someone thinking about breaking into the newspaper business? Has your advice changed over the last ten years?

A: First and foremost, you need to know how to write well, but that actually is becoming a much broader theme. You really want to be a good storyteller. You need to be able to see the narrative arc of a story, the beginning, the middle and the end, and to be able to tell that story in a variety of different media. It doesn't necessarily mean you have to have a journalism degree. There are many different educational backgrounds that can equip you to tell a good story.

Industry Snapshot

Overall Value: $56 billion

Number Employed: 380,000

Newspaper Ad Spending Growth for 2003: 1.9%

Daily Newspapers Sold: 54 million

Geographic Centers: New York, Washington, D.C., Los Angeles, Chicago

Understanding the Industry

Current trends

Readership in decline: Over the past decade, newspaper readership has declined on average by .5 percent each year. In a 2002 study by the Pew Research Center for the People and the Press, only 26 percent of respondents under 30 said they read a paper the previous day. Young adults typically get their news from the Internet or cable news. More surprising is that many people in their 40s who read newspapers 10 years ago have now stopped.

Renewed focus on the web: With their print business under pressure, newspapers are refocusing their attention on their web sites, after getting burned in the dot-com bust of 2000. Some print journalists feel the Internet has helped transform newspaper operations to meet the demands of a 24/7 news cycle. The newspaper web sites of Gannett, Knight Ridder Digital and The New York Times are among the most visited news sites, according to Nielsen/NetRatings.

Free dailies: An interesting approach to bring young adult readers back into the fold has been the emergence of free dailies like amNew York and the launch of papers in Philadelphia, Boston and New York, by European powerhouse Metro. Upwards of 80 percent of most newspapers' revenues are derived from advertising, so an easy way to boost circulation is just to give newspapers away.

Visit Vault at **www.vault.com** for insider company profiles, expert advice, career message boards, expert resume reviews, the Vault Job Board and more.

VAULT CAREER LIBRARY   17

Breaking down newspapers

Local or community papers: Many towns and cities in America still get the majority of their local news and information from newspapers. Much of the content is made up of highly targeted stories about local politics, education, crime and community events. These papers generally have small circulations, are distributed weekly or monthly and are typically free for subscribers, supported 100 percent by local advertisers.

Regional papers and metropolitan dailies: There are medium-sized and small dailies that serve an urban center and its surrounding suburbs. Generally, their circulations stand between 50,000 and 250,000. Revenue is derived from a mix of advertising and subscriptions. While most of the coverage is dedicated to local stories, there are also national and international stories based on wire sources.

National papers: Publishing newspapers that appeal to the vast and diverse expanse of America has always been a challenge, but they do exist. The top three national newspapers are *USA Today, The Wall Street Journal* and *The New York Times*.

Specialized papers: There are a variety of other newspapers serving communities ranging from labor unions to churches to associations. There is also a vibrant ethnic press in the United States serving Chinese, Hispanic, Korean and African-American communities.

Key Players

A.H. Belo Corp.
400 S. Record St.
Dallas, TX 75202-4841
Phone: 214-977-6606
Web: www.belo.com
Owns: *The Dallas Morning News, The Providence Journal*

Advance Publications
950 Fingerboard Rd.
Staten Island, NY 10305
Phone: 212-286-2860
Web: www.advance.net
Owns: *The Star-Ledger* (New Jersey), *Cleveland Plain Dealer*

Cox Newspapers
6205 Peachtree Dunwoody Rd.
Atlanta, GA 30328
Phone: 678-645-0000
Web: www.coxnews.com/cox
Owns: *Austin-American Statesman*, *Dayton Daily News*, *The Atlanta Journal-Constitution*

Dow Jones & Company
1 World Financial Center
200 Liberty St.
New York, NY 10281
Phone: 212-416-2000
Web: www.dj.com
Owns: *The Wall Street Journal*

Freedom Communications
17666 Fitch Ave.
Irvine, CA 92614-6022
Phone: 949-253-2300
Web: www.freedom.com
Owns: *The Gazette* (Colorado Springs), *Orange County Register*

Gannett Co.
7950 Jones Branch Dr.
McLean, VA 22107-0910
Phone: 703-854-6000
Web: www.gannett.com
Owns: *USA Today*

Hearst Newspapers
959 8th Ave.
New York, NY 10019
Phone: 212-649-2000
Web: www.hearst.com/newspapers
Owns: *Houston Chronicle*, *San Francisco Chronicle*, *San Antonio Express-News*, *Albany Times Union*, *Seattle Post-Intelligencer*

Visit Vault at **www.vault.com** for insider company profiles, expert advice,
career message boards, expert resume reviews, the Vault Job Board and more.

VAULT CAREER LIBRARY   19

Hollinger (U.S. Office)
401 N. Wabash Ave., Ste. 740
Chicago, IL 60611
Phone: 312-321-2299
Web: www.hollinger.com
Owns: *Chicago Sun-Times*

Knight-Ridder
50 W. San Fernando St., Ste. 1500
San Jose, CA 95113
Phone: 408-938-7700
Web: www.kri.com
Owns: *Detroit Free Press, The Philadelphia Inquirer, The Miami Herald*

Media General
333 E. Franklin St.
Richmond, VA 23219
Phone: 804-649-6000
Web: www.mediageneral.com
Owns: *Tampa Tribune, Richmond Times-Dispatch, Winston-Salem Journal*

MediaNews Group
1560 Broadway, Ste. 2100
Denver, CO 80202
Phone: 303-563-6360
Web: www.medianewsgroup.com
Owns: *The Denver Post, Salt Lake Tribune*

The E.W. Scripps Company
312 Walnut St.
Cincinnati, OH 45202
Phone: 513-977-3000
Web: www.scripps.com
Owns: *Denver Rocky Mountain News, The Commercial Appeal* (Memphis)

The New York Times Company
229 West 43rd St.
New York, NY 10036
Phone: 212-556-1234
Web: www.nytco.com
Owns: *The New York Times, Boston Globe, International Herald Tribune*

The Washington Post Company
1150 15th St. NW
Washington, DC 20071
Phone: 202-334-6000
Web: www.washpostco.com
Owns: *The Washington Post*

Tribune Co.
435 N. Michigan Ave.
Chicago, IL 60611
Phone: 312-222-9100
Web: www.tribune.com
Owns: *Chicago Tribune, The Los Angeles Times, Newsday*

The Inside Scoop

Must read

Editor & Publisher: Over 100 years old, it is the oldest journal covering all aspects of the North American newspaper industry, from journalists to advertising to technology.
www.editorandpublisher.com

I Want Media: A daily newsletter, aggregating news and headlines from around the media industry, particularly print media.
www.iwantmedia.com

International Newspaper Marketing Association: A free newsletter, providing headlines from around the newspaper industry.
www.inma.org/enewsletters.cfm

News Voyager: Online resource connecting you to almost any newspaper in the United States.
www.newspaperlinks.com/voyager.cfm

Speaking the language

Beat: A reporter's topic area, such as Courts, religion, education and specific geographic areas.

Breakout: The synopsis of the story. Key highlights of the story that stand out from the rest of the article.

Brief: A small, concise story.

Broadsheet: The size of most dailies, including *The Wall Street Journal, The New York Times, USA Today* and the *Detroit Free Press*. Folded in half, it's referred to as a tabloid.

Byline: The name of the writer, appearing at the top of an article. Credits are given to artists and photographers.

Chaser: A late edition of the newspaper in which the presses are not stopped until the plates are ready. Those pages, then, are said to be "chasing" a running press.

cq: Correct as is. A mark that lets copy editors know that something has been checked and needs no further checking.

Dateline: The city or place designation at the beginning of a story.

Embargo: A specified time when information can be released. News may be released early so that news outlets can be ready to publish or air it, but there may be a restriction on when it can be released to the public.

Gutter: The space between two columns.

Masthead: This term is used to mean three different things and can get confusing. It is used to mean 1) the name on page one, 2) the box on the editorial page with the names of top editors, or 3) the box of names, phone numbers and addresses that appears in the first few pages of the newspaper.

Pool: A designated number of reporters or one reporter covers a particular event and shares coverage with other media outlets. This is generally done for high profile events that restrict coverage to a press pool.

Proof: Any printed copy before it goes to press.

Scoop: Used as a noun, it means a story no one else has. As a verb it means to get a story first before the competition.

Sidebar: A story that accompanies the main story, showcasing a particular angle or aspect.

Skybox: Also called a teaser, the promotional boxes above the nameplate of the newspaper.

Stet: A proofreading symbol that means leave the copy as is.

Stringer: A freelance writer or photographer.

Widow: A short line of type, left at the top of a column.

Zone: Part of a newspaper's circulation area. Many times, news coverage is zoned to complement zoned advertising.

Join the club

Association of Alternate Newsweeklies
Phone: 202-822-1955
Web: aan.org

Newspaper Association of America
Phone: 703-902-1600
Web: www.naa.org

National Newspaper Publishers Association
Phone: 202-588-8764
Web: www.nnpa.org

The American Society of Newspaper Editors
Phone: 703-453-1122
Web: www.asne.org

Job leads

Journalism Jobs
www.journalismjobs.com

NewsLink
newslink.org

Newspaper JobsPage
www.freep.com/jobspage

Newsroom Jobs
www.newsroomjobs.com

The National Diversity Newspaper Job Bank
www.newsjobs.com

Visit Vault at **www.vault**.com for insider company profiles, expert advice, career message boards, expert resume reviews, the Vault Job Board and more.

VAULT CAREER LIBRARY   23

Keep Your Career Moving Forward

Special training

Believe it or not, many journalists don't have journalism degrees. Many have a liberal arts degree in English, history or philosophy. While a journalism degree can help walk you through all the nuances of the field, many in the industry value those who bring a unique background to the table in addition to their strong writing skills.

Internships at local papers near your college or working on your college paper will also provide valuable experiences to help you break into the industry. For aspiring journalists, writing for your college newspaper enables you to build a portfolio of clips that you can draw upon when you are asked for writing samples from hiring mangers.

On the business side, start building a track record. Demonstrate that you can sell ads or improve the growth of a newspaper.

Landing your first job

The best way to learn about newspapers on the creative or business side is to learn the ropes on the job. Initially the pay is low and the work is not all that glamorous, but during the first couple of years of your career, you should be focused on learning everything you can about the business to build value for yourself over the long term. Following are some tips to give you an edge to land your first job:

Be open to any job: Copy editing may not be your dream job, but it gets you in the door, so you can start meeting people and seeing how a newspaper functions. Also, once you are on the inside, people will begin to trust you. Prove yourself by accepting more responsibilities, and who knows, maybe a couple of lucky breaks will help you move up the ladder more quickly.

Cover letter and resume: You should regard your cover letter as a writing sample that will be critiqued by an editor. Take the time to make sure it is well written. If you happen to know someone in the industry, have them look it over and ask them for some pointers on what editors or sales managers are most interested in.

For those seeking sales or marketing positions, be sure to quantify your past success. How much did you boost circulation for your college newspaper?

On average, how much advertising revenue did you help generate for the newspaper where you had an internship?

Know the paper, know the city: If you go into an interview without knowing anything about the paper or the city it serves, you definitely won't be asked back for a second interview.   Editors want to see that you are passionate about the business or the city you will cover.

In sales, if you don't know anything about potential local advertisers, how are you going to convince a sales manager that you are the right person for the job?

Focus your interests: This tip may sound like it is contradicting tip number one, but giving yourself a "personal brand" will help target your job search efforts.   Don't call up a newspaper and say you will take any job; instead, ask if they have openings in the department that most interests you.   If you know you love business or finance, inquire about openings on the business desk.   If they say there is nothing open in that department right now, but the paper is looking for a copy editor, tell them you are interested.   Now you have shown them you are very focused about your career, but you are also open to learning the ropes.

Web logs (blogs): Blogs are the latest phenomenon on the Internet, enabling anyone to share their written work with the world at large.   Some are daily diaries, while others are focused on specific topics.   For aspiring journalists, blogs are an opportunity to develop your writing style, create a body of written work to share with a potential employer, and to demonstrate your initiative.   Remember to make evident your sense of judgment and objectivity.   Below are some resources to get your blog going (in as fast as 20 minutes):

- **Cyber journalist:** An online resource managed by the American Press Institute on how the Internet, media convergence and new technologies are changing journalism.   www.cyberjournalist.net

- **eblogger:** A free service that provides tools to create and manage your very own blog.   www.blogger.com

- **Moveable type publishing platform:** A publishing platform to create blogs, useful for everyone from those just starting out to those with more professional needs.   www.movabletype.org

Visit Vault at **www.vault.com** for insider company profiles, expert advice, career message boards, expert resume reviews, the Vault Job Board and more.

VAULT CAREER LIBRARY

25

Getting your career unstuck

For most people, after the first or second year, it is time to move on. This may come in the form of a promotion, or you may leave your first job for another one. At the time you feel ready to move on, there may not be a position available. The best way to move on is to just leave. Put yourself on the market. This will give you an idea if you really are as good as you think, or if there are things you still need to work on. More often than not, leaving a company gives you respect, more money and more experience at your second job.

Changing up your career may also involve weighing the benefits of working at a small paper versus a large one. At a small paper you are more likely to be given more responsibility, have the opportunity to acquire a greater variety of skills, and have greater name recognition. You also have the opportunity to become better integrated within the community you serve. The downsides are fewer resources and less pay than larger papers. Papers in larger markets also offer you more people to learn from, more prestige and the possibility of working on more high-profile stories.

As your career progresses, you should consider specializing in a specific beat. This will enhance your "personal brand" and will allow you to become an objective expert in business, health, politics or whatever field you have chosen to cover. This new course in your career will also open up opportunities beyond newspapers to write books and articles, and to speak at public forums.

Magazines

Magazines were the first true national media in America. Newspapers had been a predominantly local medium, but magazines were the first to unite people across the country with the help of the U.S. Postal system as the means of distribution. Magazines edified and entertained people from coast to coast with interests in homemaking, hunting, politics, and hundreds of other topics and hobbies.

By 1900, there were over 5,500 magazines in circulation. According to the Magazine Publishers of America, there are now well over 17,000 titles. Magazines like *Cosmopolitan*, *Atlantic Monthly* and *The Saturday Evening Post* became media fixtures in the American home by the middle of the last century. In 1923 the term "newsmagazine" was coined, with the launch of *Time*, by Henry Luce and Briton Hadden. Today magazines are facing rising production and distribution costs. Many in the industry believe their survival lies in targeting smaller and smaller niche audiences.

What makes magazines unique?

The longer format of magazines allows writers to go deeper into stories or provide more detailed information about a specific topic, whereas newspapers typically offer the latest headlines of the day. Magazines unite people with common interests like fishing, crafts, gardening or automobiles. In some instances, magazines are saved to be used as ongoing reference material in the home or office. For example, many amateur chefs and food enthusiasts save their copies of *Bon Appetit, Cooking Light* or *Food & Wine* for the recipes and cooking tips they find within their pages. While magazines are just as portable as newspapers, they are more likely to be passed around and shared with others, reaching a larger audience beyond just their subscription and newsstand circulation.

What attracts people to work for a magazine?

Overall, there are more aesthetic considerations in the development of a magazine than for a newspaper. Magazines have a personality all their own. Newspapers, on the other hand, are literally black and white, offering few frills beyond getting out the news of the day.

On the content side, many journalists savor the opportunity to sink their teeth into just one story or to stick to a specific content area. For photographers, there are far more creative opportunities in magazines than in newspapers, where photography is primarily limited to capturing images of news as it happens.

On the business side, magazines offer the opportunity to develop direct marketing campaigns to target niche audiences, rather than the one-size-fits-all marketing strategies of broadcast television. Sponsorships are also more focused on national advertisers, rather than local ones, as is common among newspapers.

Is a Career In Magazines for You?

Lifestyle

Stability is not necessarily a feature of working in magazines. Pay is very low as you start out, so it is necessary to move around a lot in order to increase your salary. Increasingly, many jobs in magazines are becoming freelance, especially on the content side, for writers, photographers, designers and illustrators.

The hours can also be crazy, especially when you are trying to meet a deadline, but working for a magazine can be very exciting. Since there always seems to be a new magazine being launched, you will be invited to many different parties. There are some people lucky enough (depending on how you look at it) to plan these posh events as their full-time jobs. As you gain responsibility, there is the potential for travel as well.

Desired skills & traits

Research: Due to their longer format and less frequent publication, magazines place a different emphasis on research than do newspapers. Not only is it important to get the facts straight, but far more detailed knowledge of subject matter is required. Research in newspapers tends to be broader, in magazines it's inclined to be more focused.

Writing: A unique writing style is necessary to capture the brand and personality of the magazine. A more personalized style also guides readers through longer stories commonly found in magazines. On the flip side, there are many magazine features that now require highly creative and "punchy" copy for features that offer readers quick pops of information.

Expertise: As magazines become more and more niche oriented, it is helpful to bring a unique area of expertise to the table, even for more general publications like *Time* or *Newsweek*. Many writers and reporters for magazines are increasingly freelance, so it is important to begin building a knowledge base in a particular area like health, business or entertainment. As a result, you can write for any magazine, rather than limiting yourself to one magazine title.

Business Skills: In such a highly competitive marketplace, where most newly launched magazines fail within the first year, business skills are crucial. Understanding demographic research, database management and direct marketing are a must. Even on the creative side, it doesn't hurt to understand the basics of business and how to better connect with your target audience.

Entrepreneurial Spirit: Last year, over 400 new titles were launched in the U.S. While established titles may not champion the entrepreneurial spirit, start-up magazines definitely do. A "can-do" attitude, good organizational skills, creativity and the ability to solve problems are all welcome traits in helping to establish a new magazine title.

Career Track

Content track

Reporters, editors and writers spend much of their time reading newspapers, surfing online and checking in with their sources looking for story ideas. It is common for them to be working on a few different stories in various stages of completion at the same time. They may be setting up interviews for one story, while writing a final draft for another. Cover stories can take months to produce, while one-page articles may take as little as a day to write.

Associate Editor or Editorial Assistant: Responsibilities for this entry-level position are largely administrative. However, there are opportunities to review manuscripts, give opinions on story proposals, line edit copy, generate story ideas, and even write for the magazine itself.

Salary Range: $25,000 to $30,000

Visit Vault at **www.vault.com** for insider company profiles, expert advice, career message boards, expert resume reviews, the Vault Job Board and more.

VAULT CAREER LIBRARY   29

Copy Editor: Reviews and edits a reporter's or writer's copy for accuracy, content, grammar, and style. Some magazines also have a fact-checker to verify statistics and other facts.

Salary Range: $35,000 to $45,000

Researcher: Responsibilities include fact-checking editorial pages and articles, as well as providing research for stories writers and reporters are developing.

Salary Range: $35,000 to $45,000

Reporter: Covers news events or a particular beat for more lifestyle oriented magazines. Pitches story ideas to the editor. Columnists, on the other hand, generally author articles based on their point of view about a specific topic and aren't necessarily encumbered by journalistic standards of objectivity.

Salary Range: $40,000 to $60,000

Managing or Senior Editor: Develops story ideas and assigns them to reporters or writers. Other responsibilities include editing copy and writing headlines, captions or in-house columns. Larger magazines may have several editors overseeing different sections of the magazine.

Salary Range: $55,000 to $70,000

Editor-in-Chief or Editorial Director: Manages the editorial department, creates the editorial guidelines and develops the budget for the editorial content.

Salary Range: $70,000 to $100,000 (or higher in some cases)

Business track

Magazines are supported by both advertising and subscription fees. Advertising, however, makes up a much larger share of the pie. The key to a successful magazine is distribution. There are several different sales functions, including selling magazines wholesale to large retailers like WalMart and Target, securing prominent placement on newsstands, and of course selling advertising in the magazines themselves. The larger the distribution, the higher the ad rates that can be demanded.

Direct marketing is also a crucial function in the highly competitive world of magazines. Lists of addresses of potential subscribers are purchased from "list brokers," who maintain lists of every different type of consumer profile a magazine publisher could imagine trying to target. Large publishers like

Time Warner have enormous subscriber lists of their own to draw from when they seek to launch new titles.

Circulation Manager: Responsible for both circulation and single-copy sales. Manages use of demographic information to create effective use of mailing lists and direct-mail marketing campaigns.

Salary Range: $75,000 to $110,000

Advertising Manager: Sells advertising space in the magazine and works with both the editorial and art departments to create an editorial climate that will generate more advertising.

Salary Range: $75,000 to $110,000

Marketing Manager: Provides descriptions of the magazine's audience, ranging from demographic and geographic to psychographic descriptions to support editorial and advertising sales efforts. Many magazines rely on studies from outside agencies, rather than having their own market research department.

Salary Range: $75,000 to $110,000

Publisher: Manages overall operational, editorial and financial goals of magazine.

Salary Range: $100,000 and up

Production track

The production of the magazine involves bringing together all the visual elements of the publication, copy for each article, as well as the advertisements. Once the magazine has been laid out and the proofs are finalized, it goes off to the print plant to be mass-produced and distributed to its subscribers.

Designers will use Quark Xpress, Pagemaker or InDesign to lay out the pages. Completed pages are proofread by the editorial department, and artistic elements like graphics and photos are reviewed by the art department. These proofs are then sent as digital files to the printer, where a printers' proof is produced for a final check by the art director and editor.

Visit Vault at **www.vault.com** for insider company profiles, expert advice,
career message boards, expert resume reviews, the Vault Job Board and more.

VAULT CAREER LIBRARY   31

Production Assistant: Entry-level position designed to be a jack of all trades, providing administrative support to entire art department or production staff.

Salary Range: $25,000 – $30,000

Photo Editor: Oversees the photo department, managing returns and licensing. Negotiates photographer's contracts and uses Photoshop to edit photos.

Salary Range: $45,000 – $70,000

Art Director: Creates the general layout and look of the magazine. Selects the photographs, graphics, colors and typefaces to promote the magazine's image, appealing to the target audience. Responsible for hiring freelance photographers, designers and illustrators, but some magazines may have their own staff.

Salary Range: $50,000 – $100,000 and up

Production Manager: Oversees the physical production of the magazine. They work with the art department to choose paper, select typefaces and colors. They schedule the printing operation from typesetting and correction to printing and distribution.

Median Salary: $55,000 – $80,000

INSIGHTS FROM INDUSTRY LEADERS

Jay McGill

Senior Vice President & Publisher, SmartMoney

In October 2003, McGill was named Senior Vice President and Publisher of *SmartMoney*. Previously, he was Vice President and Publisher of *Popular Mechanics*. He joined Hearst Magazines in 1979 as an advertising representative for *Popular Mechanics*. He has served as the Publisher of *Country Living, Sports Afield* and *Motor Boating & Sailing*.

SmartMoney debuted in March 1992, a joint venture of Dow Jones & Company and The Hearst Corporation. The magazine was founded to meet the personal financial information needs of professional Americans. It also covers technology, automotive and lifestyle subjects. Today the magazine has a paid circulation of over 800,000.

Q: How can magazines endure the digital landscape?

A: I think there's something tactile about magazines. They appeal to senses electronic media just don't appeal to. Magazines will retain their role as an entertainment and information vehicle while the Internet evolves into more of a just-in-time information vehicle.

Q: What new business opportunities are now emerging in the magazine world?

A: Just when you think that every niche has been filled, they'll find another one. What is kind of interesting is that the advancement in technology has considerably reduced the price of entry for new magazine development. Basically anyone who has a passion to crank out a magazine has the ability to see if they can find an audience with it.

The one thing that's holding magazines back now is distribution channels; reliance on the U.S. Postal Service is a big barrier to many publishers entering the marketplace, and newsstand distribution is in total shambles. It needs to be rebuilt from the ground up.

Q: Are there any new or unconventional distribution channels that you're looking at right now?

A: One of the things we're trying to do, and we're somewhat successful at it, is developing partnerships with certain organizations that will buy publications on behalf of many of their employees as a tool. For example, we're working with Merrill Lynch and their financial advisers to provide them with publications to help advise their clients. It's a very targeted approach to distribution.

The other thing we're looking at is distributing the magazine on a digital basis. We don't see this as replacing the publication. It is an opportunity for people who already subscribe or have already bought the magazine on the newsstand to also access information via the web with full search capability and links to advertiser websites or our own website for additional information.

Q: What are some of the goals for your website?

A: One of our major initiatives we launched a year and a half ago is called *"SmartMoney Select,"* a portion of the site that's subscriber-based with several levels of opportunities. What it does is package some high-powered financial tools that the user can access to track their investments, keep track of their portfolio or acquire information on certain investments. Right now we have about 15,000 subscribers; our goal is to have about 100,000 or so by the end of next year.

Visit Vault at www.vault.com for insider company profiles, expert advice, career message boards, expert resume reviews, the Vault Job Board and more.

VAULT CAREER LIBRARY

33

Understanding the Industry

Current trends

Micro Niches: While other mediums fear the fragmentation of audiences, magazines seem to have embraced the trend. There seems to be a magazine for every interest, hobby, point of view and subculture. With more than 400 titles introduced in 2003 alone, the future of the industry lies in winning the hearts and minds of core niche audiences.

Shift to Newsstands: We've all received offers to subscribe to magazines at discount prices. Magazine publishers slashed subscription rates to boost their circulation, in hopes of increasing their advertising revenue. The rising cost of mail distribution, however, has begun to undermine the economics of that strategy. Publishers are now seeking to offer lower-priced magazines at newsstands, reducing distribution costs while increasing sales and circulation.

Digital Distribution: Some publishers have been experimenting with digital distribution of magazines. To be clear, this is not simply a web site, but a digital replica of the print version. The layout looks exactly the same as the print edition. As consumers become more comfortable with reading articles online, publishers want to provide a viable digital alternative. Digital distribution is also a fraction of the cost of traditional means of distribution.

Industry Snapshot

Overall Value of Consumer Magazines: $21 billion

Overall Value of Business Magazines: $11 billion

Total Magazine Circulation: 352,000,000

Geographic Centers: New York, Chicago

Breaking Down Magazines

Magazines can be categorized by either their content or by their frequency of distribution. Typically they are distributed weekly, monthly or quarterly. Following are the basic genres of news and information-based magazines:

News: In-depth analysis and perspective on current headlines is provided by weekly news magazines like *Time, Newsweek* and *U.S. News & World Report.* They cover a wide range of topics, including politics, foreign affairs, social issues and culture. The biggest story of the week or an emerging trend is presented as the "cover story," using a multi-page layout.

Business: Coverage of the business world is big business for magazines. They cover a wide variety of topics including general business news, analysis of financial markets, personal finance and reports on specific industry sectors. Titles include *Forbes, Fortune, Money, Business 2.0* and *CIO.*

Political: Some of the first magazines were founded as political journals and editorials. Today, general news magazines provide coverage of politics, but there are magazines dedicated to the subject of politics including T*he Economist, Reason, National Review* and *the National Journal.*

Health/Fitness: As baby boomers continue their quest to stay young, and America fights its obesity problem, the interest in health issues only grows. Most health and fitness magazines are targeted to a particular gender or demographic.

Lifestyle: There are a wide variety of magazines catering to lifestyles ranging from travelers, to homemakers, to the gay community. These magazines cover many different issues through the lens of the community to whom they are reaching out. They offer advice, entertainment suggestions and ideas on how to live a fuller life.

Trades: Magazines covering specific industries like automobiles, broadcasting, pharmaceuticals or telecommunications are referred to as "trade magazines." They provide coverage of a specific industry, including articles on business issues, new product launches, executive changes and reports on industry events. Some media trade magazines include *Broadcasting & Cable, Advertising Age* and *Radio & Records.*

Visit Vault at **www.vault.com** for insider company profiles, expert advice, career message boards, expert resume reviews, the Vault Job Board and more.

VAULT CAREER LIBRARY   35

Key Players

AMI, American Media Inc.
One Park Avenue
10th Floor
New York, NY 10016
Phone: 212-545-4800
Owns: *Men's Fitness*, *SHAPE*

American Express Publishing Corporation
1120 Avenue of the Americas
New York, NY 10036
Phone: 212-382-5600
Web: www.amexpub.com
Owns: *Food & Wine*, *Travel + Leisure*

Condé Nast Publications
4 Times Square, 17th Floor
New York, NY 10036
Phone: 212-286-2860
Web: www.condenast.com

Owns: *Allure*, *Vogue*, *Wired*, *Glamour*, *GQ*, *The New Yorker*, *Vanity Fair*, *Lucky*

Crain Communications
1155 Gratiot Ave.
Detroit, MI 48207-2997
Phone: 313-446-6000
Web: www.crain.com
Owns: *Advertising Age*, *AutoWeek*, *TelevisionWeek*

Forbes Inc.
60 5th Ave.
New York, NY 10011
Phone: 212-620-2200
Web: www.forbesinc.com
Owns: *Forbes*

Gruner + Jahr AG & Co. (U.S. Office)

375 Lexington Ave., 10th Floor
New York, NY 10017
Phone: 212-499-2000
Web: www.guj.de
Owns: *Fast Company, Family Circle, Parent, Child, YM*

Hachette Filipacchi Médias (U.S. Office)

1633 Broadway, 45th Floor
New York, NY 10019
Phone: 212-767- 5322
Web: www.hachette-filipacchi.com
Owns: *Elle, Car & Driver, American Photo, Women's Day*

Hearst Magazines

959 8th Ave.
New York, NY 10019
Phone: 212-649-2000
Web: www.hearst.com/magazines
Owns: *Cosmopolitan, Good Housekeeping, Town & Country, O, The Oprah Magazine, Esquire, Popular Mechanics*

McGraw-Hill Companies

1221 Avenue of the Americas
New York, NY 10020
Phone: 212-512-2000
Web: www.mcgraw-hill.com
Owns: *BusinessWeek*

Meredith Corporation

1716 Locust St.
Des Moines, IA 50309-3023
Phone: 515-284-3000
Web: www.meredith.com
Owns: *Better Homes and Gardens, Ladies' Home Journal, MORE*

National Geographic Society

1145 17th St. NW
Washington, DC 20036-4688
Phone: 202-857-7000
Web: www.nationalgeographic.com
Owns: *National Geographic*

Visit Vault at **www.vault.com** for insider company profiles, expert advice,
career message boards, expert resume reviews, the Vault Job Board and more.

VAULT CAREER LIBRARY

37

PRIMEDIA
745 5th Ave.
New York, NY 10151
Phone: 212-745-0100
Web: www.primedia.com
Owns: *Motor Trend*, *Soap Opera Digest*

Rodale
33 East Minor Street
Emmaus, PA 18098
Phone: 610-967-5171
Web: rodale.com
Owns: *Men's Health*, *Organic Living*, *Organic Style*, *Men's Health*

The Washington Post Company
1150 15th St. NW
Washington, DC 20071
Phone: 202-334-6000
Web: www.washpostco.com
Owns: *Newsweek*

Time, Inc.
1271 Avenue of the Americas
New York, NY 10020-1393
Phone: 212-522-1212
Web: www.timeinc.com
Owns: *Time, Entertainment Weekly, People, Sports Illustrated, Fortune*

U.S. News & World Reports
1050 Thomas Jefferson St. NW
Washington, DC 20007-3837
Phone: 202-955-2000
Web: www.usnews.com
Owns: *U.S. News & World Reports*

Wenner Media
1290 Avenue of the Americas
New York, NY 10104-0298
Phone: 212-484-1616
Owns: *Rolling Stone, Men's Journal, US Weekly*

The Inside Scoop

Must read

Circulation Management: Trade magazine focusing on circulation and marketing trends in magazines.
www.circman.com

Folio: Trade magazine providing a comprehensive perspective and analysis on issues facing the magazine industry.
www.foliomag.com

M10 Report: A multidimensional information resource providing magazine professionals with business solutions to promote greater dialogue between buyers and sellers.
www.m10report.com

I Want Media: A free online newsletter providing links to articles from around the media industry, especially the print media.
www.iwantmedia.com

Speak the language

Alley: White space (margin) between columns of type and/or graphics.

Average Issue Audience (Readership): Projected number of people who have read or looked into an "average issue" of a magazine.

Call-outs: Brief passages of text lifted from within the publication placed in larger type size (and occasionally font) to gain attention.

Circulation: The number of distributed copies of a magazine.

Composite Image: A photograph or other graphic image that is made of a combination of multiple images.

Composition: The demographic profile of a magazine.

Duplication: The percentage of readers that two or more magazines have in common.

Exclusive Readers: Readers who read one magazine but not another.

Impressions: The gross sum of all media exposures (numbers of people/homes) without regard to duplication.

Visit Vault at **www.vault.com** for insider company profiles, expert advice,
career message boards, expert resume reviews, the Vault Job Board and more.

VAULT CAREER LIBRARY   **39**

Issue Life: The length of time it takes a magazine to be read by the maximum measurable audience.

List Broker: A list specialist hired by a magazine to make the necessary arrangements to use other companies' customer lists for their direct marketing efforts.

Masthead: The section of a magazine detailing such information as title, address and staff.

Pass-Along (Secondary) Readers: Readers who obtain the magazine secondhand, thus not purchasing it.

Rate Base: The circulation of a magazine upon which advertising space rates are based, which may or may not be guaranteed by the publisher.

Recency: The advertising scheduling tactic delivering ad messages immediately prior to purchase decisions.

Return on Investment (ROI): The sales return on the advertising expenditures invested in media.

Volumetrics: Total product usage or spending by a particular magazine audience on a specific product/service.

Photo Plate: A light sensitive printing plate. The plate is developed like film, then used on a printing press.

Pica: A unit of measurement equal to twelve (12) points or one sixth (1/6) of an inch. Used by designers and other graphics professional for its precision.

Style Sheet: A page or group of pages designating the typefaces to be used in a design, e.g. in headlines, captions and body text.

Join the club

American Society of Magazine Editors
Phone: (212) 872-3710
Web: www.magazine.org/Editorial/

Magazine Publishers of America
Phone: (212) 872-3710
Web: www.magazine.org

Job leads

Journalism Jobs

www.journalismjobs.com

Magazine Publishers of America Job Bank

jobs.magazine.org/

MediaBistro

www.mediabistro.com

Keep Your Career Moving Forward

Special training

Generally speaking, there are no specific degrees necessary for a career in magazines. Many in the industry have a liberal arts degree, and some may have a degree in journalism. As a targeted medium, magazines attract people from a variety of backgrounds. They bring their expertise to the industry as writers and reporters from finance, healthcare, cooking, gardening and practically any number of other disciplines you can imagine.

On the photography and design side, formal training at an art school or a university art program is recommended.

For those interested in a marketing or sales role, a degree in marketing or business is not necessary, but certainly wouldn't hurt.

Landing your first job

Yes, it is true that hundreds of new titles are launched every year, but unfortunately most end in failure just after the first year. The magazine industry is highly competitive, and so is trying to land your first job in this field.

Freelance: Temporary work is very common in the magazine industry. Freelancing doesn't offer you the security and stability of a staff job, but it gets your foot in the door. As you start out, it enables you to try different things without committing to any for the long term. And working at several different magazines will help you to build your network of contacts to find more permanent work. Freelancing also fills out your resume, and adds to your experience.

Visit Vault at **www.vault.com** for insider company profiles, expert advice, career message boards, expert resume reviews, the Vault Job Board and more.

VAULT CAREER LIBRARY   41

Your portfolio: Writers obviously will be asked for samples of their work. As you select samples, try to target the content to the magazine where you are applying. For example, if you are applying to a health magazine, try to include some health-related articles as part of your standard samples.

A portfolio for design or photography positions aren't necessary for entry-level positions, but become more and more important as you progress through your career. As you gather experience, it is a good idea to start building your portfolio and to push your proverbial creative envelope. As with writing samples, you should include examples of your work that relate to the type of magazines where you would like to work.

Study the magazine: Don't walk into an interview without knowing the magazine backwards and forwards. Before the interview, buy the past two or three issues and study them! You are meeting with people that built this magazine. Let them know that you have an interest in what they do.

Getting your career unstuck

It is not uncommon to spend less than one year at your first job. The best way to get ahead in magazines and to increase your salary is to move around. It helps you gain experience, responsibility and respect.

Many magazine writers and photographers have turned to freelance, or more accurately, have been left no alternative but to freelance. Once again, freelance doesn't offer stability, but it could be the beginning of your own business. Working on your own will enable you to work on a variety of projects, enriching your career with different experiences that working at the same magazine may not be able to offer you.

Radio

Radio was the first electronic mass medium, bringing live news events as they happened into millions of homes for the first time. Still unsure of its impact, Orson Welles duped millions of listeners into thinking Martians were invading earth in 1938. Charles Collingwood, Eric Sevareid and Edward R. Murrow brought millions of Americans to the front lines of war, sending back live reports from Europe during World War II.

Radio was quickly adopted by Americans: 90 percent of homes owned one by 1930. In that year, radio personality Lowell Thomas gave birth to radio news when he began reading the news on air. At first, newspapers tried to fight this trend, citing copyright laws, but they were eventually overruled when the courts determined that no one could own the news, and the factual content was part of the public domain. The Golden Age of radio was eclipsed by the advent of television in the 1950s, forcing it to reinvent itself from the primary electronic medium for news and entertainment into a local medium for news, talk and music.

What makes Radio unique?

Radio is a mass medium, but it creates a one-on-one relationship between the announcer and the listener. The listener is allowed to visualize a story for themselves, becoming absorbed in their own imagination as they are guided by a storyteller. For this reason, radio has been often referred to as "the theater of the mind."

Radio is probably the least expensive of all media to consume, thereby truly reaching out to a mass audience. The phenomenon of talk radio also promotes a diversity of voices and allows the average man or woman the opportunity to be heard in a public forum. The unique features of radio provide insight in to what is on the minds of Americans. It's no surprise that radio talk show hosts are regularly interviewed by television broadcasters when major news events like the attacks of September 11th occur, in order to understand the common person's perspective.

What attracts people to work In radio?

Like newspapers, every day is different and there is a focus on serving local communities. Radio provides a more personal connection to the audience than print. The nature of the medium promotes a sense of immediacy –

getting reaction from the community as news happens. Of course, if you have a voice like velvet, it certainly won't hurt your chances of landing an on-air gig!

On the business side, radio offers a similar opportunity to that of newspapers, in working with local sponsors. Radio also enables advertisers to target niche audiences, and offers greater flexibility to refine their marketing messages than they can in print. Once an ad hits the presses, there's no turning back, but it is technically possible to change a radio spot throughout the course of the day.

Is a Career In Radio for You?

Lifestyle

The news never stops, so reporters, anchors and producers find themselves working a variety of different shifts and will work long hours to cover major news stories. There is also considerable pressure to meet deadlines. The plus side of a hectic schedule is that every day is truly different.

Pay is generally lower than in television broadcasting, thus many radio broadcasters move into television by their 30s, or leave the field altogether if they haven't advanced to a more senior level by then.

Desired skills & traits

Hands-on Experience: A degree in journalism certainly doesn't hurt your chances of landing a job in radio news, but real world experience is a must if you want to rise above the competition. You will be looked upon more favorably if you worked at your college radio station, had an internship or gained experience in another news medium than someone who didn't.

Understanding Technology: In today's media world, whether stated or not, all job descriptions include a working understanding of technology. Particularly at smaller radio stations, the ease of new digital technologies has forced producers, anchors and reporters to assume greater responsibility for producing and editing their own stories without the help of a broadcast technician or editor. Learning about new technologies and new computer programs will be an ongoing process throughout your career.

Communication Skills: It goes without saying, there is enormous importance placed on written and verbal skills. For those interested in on-air positions, a pleasant voice and solid delivery skills are essential to a successful career in radio.

Career Track

Content track

The primary function of the editorial staff is to gather and report the news. Each morning, they have a meeting to pitch story ideas and to assign resources to stories to be covered that day. They monitor wires, call on their sources and read a variety of print media to find stories.

Much of the content in radio is interview-driven, and because there are no visual elements, a premium is placed on telling a story through the written word. Anchors conduct interviews in the studio by phone, live on the air, with a newsmaker like a local politician, civic leader or another member of the community. Reporters will conduct interviews as part of their stories and will also collect sound bites from "Man on the Street" (MOS) interviews to be used in taped stories or as part of live interview segments.

Desk Assistant: For those just getting their start in radio, desk assistants are a "jack of all trades," helping to research stories, set up interviews and even write copy for news readers. Generally, most start out at smaller stations, where there is an opportunity to gain more hands-on experience than at a station in a larger market.

Median Salary: $20,000

Writer: Writes copy for announcers and anchors, as well as introductions for packages produced by reporters. Once again, at smaller stations with fewer resources, anchors most likely write much of their own scripts.

Median Salary: $23,000

Producer: More likely found at larger stations, producers develop the rundown for live broadcasts and book interviews for live interview broadcasts or talk shows.

Median Salary: $26,000

Visit Vault at **www.vault.com** for insider company profiles, expert advice, career message boards, expert resume reviews, the Vault Job Board and more.

VAULT CAREER LIBRARY   45

Assignment Editor: Cruises the wires, the fire department and police scanners and consults community sources, looking for stories or breaking news like fires and shootings. The assignment editor will also help write certain stories, particularly those from the wires, as well as copy to introduce reporter packages.

Median Salary: $25,000

Reporter: Goes out into the community to investigate leads and news tips, gathers information for stories and conducts interviews. Once a reporter has gathered all the elements for his story, he writes a script and produces his package or segment. Reporters also report live from news events.

Median Salary: $26,000

Anchors: Monitors the wires for stories, writes copy, introduces stories by reporters, provides perspective for breaking news, conducts live interviews and delivers the news to the community of listeners.

Median Salary: $25,000

Host: Similar to an anchor, but generally associated with a live broadcast made up of in-studio interviews or call-ins from listeners.

Commentators: Provide opinions or editorials about news events or issues facing a local community.

Assistant News Director: Manages day-to-day news gathering and production operations.

Median Salary: $25,000

News Director: Provides editorial direction for the station, develops budgets and oversees the assignment of resources for news coverage.

Median Salary: $31,000

General Manager: Provides overall leadership for editorial, sales and promotion for a station.

Median Salary: Varies widely depending on the size of the station and market.

Business track

The two primary functions on the business side are driving revenue for the broadcasts through the sale of advertisements, and maintaining the overall financial health of the station. This involves identifying sales targets, as well as developing budgets.

The sales staff develops lists of potential sponsors called "leads." They pitch advertising opportunities to sponsors and close deals to sell time, signing contracts with advertisers and sponsors. Some of the sponsorships include prerecorded commercials, testimonials and 30/30s (half commercials and half content related to the sponsor). For example, a pharmaceutical may run a 30-second spot, followed by a 30-second health tip.

Public and community radio stations are supported by underwriters and donations from listeners. The key to building a career in radio sales is continuing to develop a better and better track record. Some may argue it's all about the numbers, but a high degree of creativity is needed to develop and sell sponsorship opportunities that others may not see.

There are two basic types of sales positions, local sales and national sales. Local sales reps primarily go after local sponsors like car dealerships, restaurants, lawyers, and a flurry of other small businesses trying to market their services to the local community. National sales reps manage the accounts of national sponsors seeking to target their products or services to local communities.

Below is a typical career path for sales in radio:

- Entry-level: Sales Assistant (Median entry-level salary is $20,000)
- Mid-level: Account Executive
- Senior-level: Sales Manager
- Executive-level: General Sales Manager

Production track

Once the sound bites, written copy and reporter packages have been gathered, it's up to the production and technical staff to tie the content together into a seamless broadcast. Some reporters will edit their own packages, but larger stations may still use editors. Broadcast technicians are responsible for operating the transmitters, overall maintenance of the broadcast signal and taking in feeds.

Visit Vault at **www.vault.com** for insider company profiles, expert advice, career message boards, expert resume reviews, the Vault Job Board and more.

VAULT CAREER LIBRARY   47

The production staff not only produces news content, but almost, if not all, of the commercials for sponsors. Unlike television, most of the commercials sold on radio stations are produced by the radio station itself, because the cost of production is so low and is regarded as a service to the sponsor.

Many radio stations have now gone digital. New technologies have simplified the production of radio packages to the extent that many reporters now produce their own stories on their own home computer.

Below is a typical career path for production in radio:

- Entry-level: Production Assistant (median salary is $20,000)
- Mid-level: Editor, Broadcast Technician, Associate Director
- Senior-level: Director, Engineer

INSIGHTS FROM INDUSTRY LEADERS

Charles Osgood

Anchor, CBS Radio

For almost 40 years, the voice of Charles Osgood has graced the airwaves of American radio. His daily news commentary, *The Osgood File*, is broadcast on the CBS Radio Network. In 1994, he succeeded Charles Kuralt as anchor of *CBS News Sunday Morning*. He is also the author of six books, including *See You on the Radio* and *The Osgood Files*. His honors and awards include three Peabody Awards and three Emmy Awards.

Q: What's the draw to radio after almost 40 years?

A: Well, it obviously beats working for a living. It's fun to meet the people I meet and do the things I do. It has a lot going for it as a livelihood. It is really more fun than anything else I can think of that I might possibly do.

If I didn't do this, I wouldn't miss it because I wouldn't know that it was a possibility for me. I think that's how a lot of people choose career paths; for every door you open, you close a lot of other doors behind you. You start off with infinite possibilities, and then as you make choices, you close off your options. What you choose to do as a career automatically involves eliminating other possibilities.

Q: It's very different for people entering the broadcast journalism industry today, but what shouldn't be forgotten about the business?

A: The thing to keep in mind is basically what you're doing is storytelling. You have to talk to an audience, whether they can see you or just hear you, and you have to treat them with respect.

I never took a broadcasting course. I never took a journalism course. I majored in economics in college; Fordham had an excellent journalism program, but I didn't go that way. They did have a radio station, and that was what I did between classes. I hung out there because I just liked the idea of being there. So what was supposed to be a side thing turned out to be the main event for me. When I graduated from Fordham in 1954, I went to work at a radio station – actually, I started before graduation day, and I've been mostly employed since then.

Q: Where do you get your inspiration from for the Osgood Files?

A: In radio you are talking to one person at a time. It doesn't matter how many millions are listening, they hear it one at a time. You're just talking to one person, probably sitting in a car, maybe in their kitchen or when their alarm clock goes off. You have to remember what their situation is and what they might like to know about what's going on in the world.

The great thing about doing news as opposed to just sitting around on your bum every day is that it is a constant source of material. Things keep happening in the world and you can sort through it to find what might interest you and therefore might also interest someone else.

You have to apply journalistic standards, but that's not something you have to go to journalism school to do. I've never even taken a course in writing or any of the other things I do, and some people might say that explains a lot. On the other hand, I think a certain amount of creativity gets drummed out of you. I think somebody might look at what I would do and say, "No, that's not what people want." Maybe they are right, but they also might want it if they had it. Don't anticipate a censor too soon. Do things the best way you can think of to do it, and then later if you have to make a change, go ahead and do it.

Visit Vault at **www.vault.com** for insider company profiles, expert advice, career message boards, expert resume reviews, the Vault Job Board and more.

VAULT CAREER LIBRARY 49

Understanding the Industry

Current trends

Consolidation: Since the Telecommunications Act of 1996, the radio industry has experienced the most consolidation of any media sector. Critics argue that consolidation has reduced choices for consumers and has diluted programming. For example, Clear Channel owns 14 stations in San Diego alone. Radio executives, on the other hand, say consolidation has helped save many radio stations from bankruptcy, and has brought higher quality programming to smaller markets that would not have otherwise been able to afford it.

Indecency Debate: Who could have imagined the furor over Janet Jackson's "wardrobe malfunction" during the Super Bowl in 2004? The indecency debate has become a hot political issue and the radio industry has been caught in its crosshairs. In March of 2004, Congress passed the Broadcast Decency Enforcement Act, raising fines against violators by nearly four times. The FCC has targeted "shock jocks" like Howard Stern, causing radio powerhouse Clear Channel to drop the Stern broadcast from its stations altogether. Stern has recently signed an unprecedented deal with satellite radio to the tune of $500 million.

Digital Radio: The bulk of radio's revenues, and audience, are still driven by its over-the-air broadcasts, but Internet radio stations and satellite radio services, like XM Satellite Radio, continue to grow. Digital formats enable consumers to listen to music and other programs when convenient for them, and, of course, without commercials. There are countless Internet radio stations serving every type of audience imaginable. The advent of television forced radio to reinvent itself, moving towards music and news programming. It's still too early to speculate on the long-term impression digital technologies will leave on broadcast radio.

Breaking Down Radio

Talk Radio: Radio's answer to the newspaper editorial is talk radio. Yes, there are shock jocks like Howard Stern, those doling out their "tough love" advice like Dr. Laura, and still others who have made a name for themselves slanting the headlines of the day with their own political views. Most would argue conservative talk radio has the upper hand, but the liberal side of the aisle is now countering this programming with the struggling talk network,

Air America. Talk radio provides a soap box not only for radio personalities, but also for anyone who wants to call in with an opinion, making radio one of the first great democratic mediums.

Network Radio: Affiliates in radio have a far looser relationship with their network than they do in television. They have much more control over when they air network programming, if they even choose to do so. CBS and ABC are just about the last major broadcasters to provide network news programming. CNN and Fox News have recently started new radio networks to extend their brand beyond their television outlets.

Local Radio: The vast majority of news content in radio is produced locally and focuses on covering local stories. For some communities, radio is the only source of local news, particularly in rural areas.

Public Radio: As in television, the Corporation for Public Broadcasting backs a publicly funded radio network, National Public Radio (or NPR as it is more commonly known). It provides national programming, like old standbys Morning Edition and Fresh Air, with hundreds of affiliates covering local communities that might not have otherwise have had a news radio presence.

Industry Snapshot

Overall Value: $20 billion

Number Employed: 143,000

Ad Spending Growth for 2003: 1%

Total Number of Stations: 13,300

Geographic Centers: New York, Chicago, Los Angeles, Texas

Visit Vault at **www.vault.com** for insider company profiles, expert advice,
career message boards, expert resume reviews, the Vault Job Board and more.

VAULT CAREER LIBRARY   51

Key Players

ABC, Inc.
77 W. 66th St.
New York, NY 10023-6298
Phone: 212-456-7777
Web: www.abcradio.com
Owns: More than 70 radio stations.

Bloomberg Radio
499 Park Ave.
New York, NY 10022
Phone: 212-318-2000
Web: www.bloomberg.com/radio/
Syndicates business reports to 840 affiliates worldwide.

Citadel Broadcasting
7201 W. Lake Mead Blvd., Ste. 400
Las Vegas, NV 89128
Phone: 702-804-5200
Web: www.citadelbroadcasting.com
Owns: More than 200 radio stations.

Clear Channel Communications
200 E. Basse Rd.
San Antonio, TX 78209
Phone: 210-822-2828
Web: www.clearchannel.com
Number 1 radio station owner in the U.S. It owns, operates, programs or sells airtime for over 1,200 radio stations.

Cox Radio
6205 Peachtree Dunwoody Rd.
Atlanta, GA 30328
Phone: 678-645-0000
Web: www.coxradio.com
Owns: 80 radio stations.

Cumulus Media
3535 Piedmont Rd., Bldg. 14, Fl. 14
Atlanta, GA 30305
Phone: 404-949-0700
Web: www.cumulus.com
Second largest owner of radio stations in U.S. with over 300 stations.

Emmis Communications
40 Monument Circle, Ste. 700
Indianapolis, IN 46204
Phone: 317-266-0100
Web: www.emmis.com
Owns: 27 radio stations.

Entercom Communications
401 City Ave., Ste. 409
Bala Cynwyd, PA 19004
Phone: 610-660-5610
Web: www.entercom.com
Owns: More than 100 radio stations.

Fisher Communications
100 4th Ave. North, Ste. 440
Seattle, WA 98109
Phone: 206-404-7000
Web: www.fsci.com
Owns: 27 radio stations.

Infinity Broadcasting
1515 Broadway, 46th Floor
New York, NY 10036
Phone: 212-846-3939
Web: www.infinityradio.com
Owns: 185 radio stations.

National Public Radio
635 Massachusetts Ave. NW
Washington, DC 20001-3753
Phone: 202-513-2000
Web: www.npr.org
Owns: 680 member stations.

Westwood One
40 West 57th St.
New York, NY 10019
Phone: 212-641-2000
Web: www.westwoodone.com
Broadcasts programming to more than 7,700 radio stations.

Visit Vault at www.vault.com for insider company profiles, expert advice,
career message boards, expert resume reviews, the Vault Job Board and more.

VAULT CAREER LIBRARY   53

The Inside Scoop

Must read

Radio Ink: Magazine covering the latest business, programming and marketing trends in radio.
www.radioink.com

Radio & Records: Information company serving the decision makers of the radio and record industries via print, online and seminars.
www.radioandrecords.com

ShopTalk: TVSpy's daily newsletter dedicated to covering the broadcast news industry.
www.tvspy.com

Speak the language

Actuality: Also known as a sound bite. A recorded segment of a newsmaker speaking.

Announcer: Person who serves as the anchor, reading news briefs and introducing reporters' segments.

Clock: The schedule of a broadcast hour, in which each segment is precisely scheduled. Resembles a pie chart.

Cut: Tape containing the recording of a voicer, wrap, actuality or nat sound, generally fed by the networks to their affiliates.

Hourly: Network newscast beginning at the top of the hour.

In Cue (IQ): First words recorded on a cut.

Lead: First sentence of a news story, also called a "hook."

Live Shot: Report introduced by an anchor of a reporter live at a news scene.

Lockout: Final words of a report spoken by a journalist in which the journalist's name and station call letters or frequency are given.

Man on the Street (MOS): Interviews with people chosen at random in a public place to ask their opinions about a current news event.

Out Cue (OQ): The last words recorded on a cut.

Reader: Script of a news story read by the anchor in which no actualities are to be played.

Voicer: Recording of a story read by a reporter without an actuality. Reader by a reporter is called a "voicer."

Script: Written-out version of a news story, the text of which is read on the air.

Slug: Title of a script; used for reference purposes.

Sounder: Recorded tune used to introduce segments of the broadcast, such as at the beginning of a traffic report or sports.

Spot: Recorded commercial advertisement.

30/30: An advertorial in radio, in which a sponsor pays for 60 seconds of air time. The first 30 seconds are content related to the sponsor's product or service, followed by a 30 second commercial for the sponsor.

Stringer: A person who pitches stories to a station or is called upon to help cover a story because of his particular expertise. Stringers have an even less formal relationship to a station than a freelancer.

Zinger or Kicker: Unusual and generally humorous feature story often placed at the end of a newscast.

Join the club

American Federation of Television and Radio Artists
Phone: 212-532-0800
Web: www.aftra.org

American Women in Radio and Television (AWRT)
Phone: (703) 506-3290
Web: www.awrt.org

National Association of Broadcasters
Phone: 202-429-5300
Web: www.nab.org

Radio and Television News Directors Association
Phone: (202) 659-6510
Web: www.rtnda.org

Visit Vault at **www.vault.com** for insider company profiles, expert advice,
career message boards, expert resume reviews, the Vault Job Board and more.
VAULT CAREER LIBRARY
55

Job leads

Journalism Jobs
www.journalismjobs.com

National Association of Broadcasters Job Bank
www.nab.org

RTNDA Job Bank
www.rtnda.org

Radio 411
radio411.com/classifieds.htm

Radio Ink
www.radioink.com

TVandRadioJobs
www.tvandradiojobs.com

Youth Radio
Nonprofit radio station based in Berkeley, CA, covering issues of interest to America's young adults, as well as providing training to aspiring radio broadcasters.
www.youthradio.org

Keep Your Career Moving Forward

Special training

Attending a journalism school or a broadcast school provides aspiring broadcasters the opportunity to develop a demo tape. As with other media sectors, a journalism degree isn't required, but can only enhance your skills. While journalism schools focus more on the theoretical practices of journalism, broadcast schools focus on more of the vocational aspects of broadcast journalism.

Whether you are interested in on-air, writing, producing or sales, working at your college radio station is a great way to get your feet wet. The experience will provide you with an understanding of the basic functions of a radio station and will help you decide if this is the career for you. Internships at local radio stations near your university are also a valuable way to gain experience, and also enable you to build contacts for your future job search.

For those interested in on-air positions, internships or working at your college radio station are easy ways to develop your demo tape to send out to potential employers. Don't overlook public radio stations or radio shows that are independently produced as well.

Landing your first job

Radio is highly competitive, and some may argue even more so over the last few years with the rapid consolidation of the industry.

Ugly duckling opportunities: Go for the jobs no one else really wants – late shifts, working weekends, or less popular beats like education or business. While not a glamorous entry into radio, it's a way into the business.

It takes 30 'No's' to get one 'Yes' in sales: If you are good at sales, you will always have a job. What company wouldn't hire someone who will make them money? If you are starting out, sales can be a great way to break into the business. In smaller markets, a sales position will still allow you the opportunity to pursue a job on the production side, or in another department.

Expand your technical knowledge: Over the last five years, the radio industry has gone digital, making many technical positions obsolete, and making it easier for non-technical staff to edit their own pieces or to manage the overall production of programming. The more comfortable you are with using nonlinear editing equipment, the more attractive you are to potential employers.

Your voice: Aspiring to be on air? You better have a beautiful voice, great delivery and solid enunciation; otherwise, consider something behind the scenes. A demo tape of your work will be required by news directors. Choose a variety of pieces: long, short, live and taped, to demonstrate the range of your abilities. If you are still in school, consult the advice of a theater professor, or consider getting a small part in a play to start developing your voice.

Getting your career unstuck

Many radio professionals typically start off in a smaller market to gain experience, and then move on to larger markets for higher-paying positions. As some reporters begin to burn out from the grind of covering daily news, they begin to specialize. When you are at the point to focus your career on covering a specific field, be sure that what you are passionate about is something radio stations have a need for, or sponsors find attractive.

Visit Vault at **www.vault.com** for insider company profiles, expert advice, career message boards, expert resume reviews, the Vault Job Board and more.

VAULT CAREER LIBRARY   **57**

There is also no reason you can't make lateral moves into different career paths within radio. Obviously, the leap from producing to reporting is smaller than that from sales to reporting, but anything is possible. It is also common for anchors and reporters to make the transition into television.

TV News

CHAPTER 5

Broadcast television burst forth in the late 1940s, growing out of the tradition of broadcast radio. In fact, it was first regarded as "radio with pictures." It soon developed into a form all its own. It brought groundbreaking events into millions of Americans' living rooms, from Edward R. Murrow's look at the life of migrant workers to Walter Cronkite reporting from the middle of the Vietnam war zone to the live-television assassination of Lee Harvey Oswald by Jack Ruby.

Since its birth over 60 years ago, television news has grown to become the voice of local communities throughout America, and national broadcasts have helped make our vast country seem smaller. Over the last two decades, the emergence of cable television, led by the pioneering efforts of Ted Turner's CNN in 1980, has grown to deliver news 24/7.

What makes television news unique?

Broadcast television has enabled interview subjects to share their story in their own words. Sometimes moving images speak for themselves without the aid of a professional journalist's words. Broadcast stories have made us swell with pride, shed a tear or bust a gut. Television has enabled a mass audience to witness history first hand – to view news as it happens.

Through the years, television journalism has provided Hollywood with inspiration, ranging from dramas like *Broadcast News* to revealing looks at the industry based on true stories, like *The Insider*, to comedies like *Anchorman*. Why are Americans so fascinated by television news? For the same reason so many people pursue a career in this business – the combination of the star power generated by a visual broadcast medium and the ability of video journalism to capture the raw emotion of a story.

What attracts people to work in television news?

Many television journalists love the rush of reporting live news events and being able to share those images with viewers at home. Video enables journalists to capture the sights, sounds and details of a moment like no other medium.

Most news broadcasts are live, adding to the pressure of the environment and the immediacy with which news is delivered to a mass audience. Television news shares many of the same characteristics of other journalistic disciplines, but it is perceived as the most glamorous. At the national level, your work can be shared with a larger audience than newspapers, magazines or radio can attract.

Is a Career In Television News for You?

Lifestyle

Just because it's your day off doesn't mean the world stops. News doesn't always come at the most convenient time in your life when you are a television journalist. Ask any veteran journalist about sacrifices made: missed birthdays, anniversaries and vacations are possibilities, and personal relationships are often put on the back burner as well.

The exciting part of working in television news is that every day is different. You are constantly meeting interesting people and learning about new ideas. One day you may be covering a court case, and the next day you might be skydiving.

The starting salaries in television news are extremely low. It is definitely one of those careers you pursue because you love it and because you believe you can make a difference in the world through your work. That doesn't mean the money won't come eventually. As with anything else in life, if you are good at what you do, you will be rewarded. It just takes some time in television news.

Building a career in television news has traditionally required moving around a lot. Most people start off in very small markets where the pay is low and someone with no experience has a shot at landing their first job. To make more money, most people hop around the country, jumping to larger and larger markets. This strategy is definitely true of people who want to be on air. Those behind the scenes also move around a lot as well, but have more opportunities to start out in larger markets or at the national level. If you don't think you can handle living in Paducah, Kentucky for a year, you better think twice about a career in television news.

Desired skills & traits

Persistence: There is a fine line between being annoying and being persistent, but it's a line journalists must walk every day. Getting an exclusive or landing a "get interview" takes many long hours of persuasion, negotiation and patience. Many people get into the business for the rush of beating a competitor to a big interview or convincing a reluctant interview subject to share their story.

Perspective: Whether you are an assignment editor, reporter, editor, photographer or a producer, understanding "the big picture" will keep you from being overwhelmed by details when you are producing a story. Producing for television is a team effort and each role is crucial in the creation of the final product, the newscast.

An assignment editor needs to prioritize the stories of the day in terms of resources, a producer needs to understand how a story flows with the other stories in the newscast, and reporters need to convey both sides of a story, offering a balanced perspective to viewers.

Storytelling: Simply gathering the who, what, when, where and why of a story won't make you a great television journalist. To take yourself to the next level, you need to be able to convey the information you've gathered via a compelling story that will resonate with your intended audience.

Presentation Skills: Much of television is about presentation. It is, after all, a visual medium. While looks aren't everything, they count for a heck of a lot. Always seek out the extra detail or finishing touch to be sure to tie all your elements together into a story that flows seamlessly. A good eye goes a long way in television.

Communication Skills: Despite what track you are on, it goes without saying that great communications skills are a must. If you want to be an on-air report or anchor, a clear and fluid delivery is just as important as your writing skills. If you want to become a producer, a catchy and concise writing style will help you rise above the rest.

Visit Vault at **www.vault.com** for insider company profiles, expert advice, career message boards, expert resume reviews, the Vault Job Board and more.

VAULT CAREER LIBRARY

61

Career Track

Content track

When most people think of pursuing a career in television news, they think of positions in newsgathering or production. Newsgathering involves looking for story ideas, researching facts, developing sources and any other aspect of gathering information. Once the facts have been gathered, stories, segments and newscasts are produced by reporters, producers and editors.

Production track

An often overlooked, but critical group of people in television are the engineers and technicians. They build and maintain the technology that enables the broadcasting of video news gathered by reporters and producers. For example, live truck operators broadcast live shots from remote locations by beaming a satellite signal back to the station. Directors and associate directors are in charge of the technical elements of a live broadcast and direct the newscast according to the rundown developed by the producer. Graphic artists design animations and graphics as additional visual elements to help tell a story.

At this time, television stations are undergoing a significant change in terms of technology, shifting from analog broadcast equipment to digitally-based technologies. As a result, many broadcast technician jobs like camera operators, editors and some maintenance engineers are being replaced by these new digital technologies. Robotic cameras are increasingly being used in studios, eliminating the need for camera operators. Nonlinear editing systems are enabling producers to edit their own video, thus reducing the need for editors. In light of managing delivery systems based on bits and bytes, some in the industry go so far as to say it is now more appropriate to refer to broadcast engineers as IT managers.

Below is a typical career path for production in television:

- Entry-level: Production Assistant (Median entry-level salary is $20,000)
- Mid-level: Editor, Broadcast Technician, Associate Director, Live Truck Operator, Graphics Designer
- Senior-level: Director, Engineer, Vice President

Business track

Advertising Sales: Some like to believe television is free, but throughout its existence, broadcast TV has been paid for by advertisers, who then pass on that marketing cost to consumers in the form of higher priced goods and services. Stations affiliated with networks can only sell commercials at the top and bottom of the hour during network broadcasts, like primetime programming. Local stations' most lucrative source of revenue is the commercials that run throughout their local news broadcasts.

Ad rates are based on Nielsen ratings. They are determined at least twice a year (four times a year for major markets) during sweeps (also known as "the book"), which occur in November, February, May and July. A traditional television season for broadcasters begins with the new fall line-up in September and lasts through the season finales in May.

The bulk of broadcast advertising is sold in the "upfront market" in May, in which advertisers are given a discount for buying advertising on an annual basis. Spots that aren't sold in the upfront are sold throughout the rest of the year in the "scatter market." Increasing competition from cable is causing broadcasters to rethink their decades-old scheduling approach. They are now trying to program new shows, particularly reality programming, during the summer months, which had been previously dominated by "repeats."

The value of advertising is also determined by "dayparts." The day is divided up into various parts, based on the size and type of audience watching television at that time. The most lucrative daypart is primetime, when television draws the largest audience, while "the overnight" is the least desirable. A typical day is broken down as follows:

Early Morning: 5 a.m. to 7 a.m.

Morning: 7 a.m. to 9 a.m.

Daytime: 9 a.m. to 5 p.m.

Early Evening: 5 p.m. to 7 p.m.

Early Prime: 7 p.m. to 8 p.m.

Primetime: 8 p.m. to 11 p.m.

Late Night: 11 p.m. to 2 a.m.

Overnight: 2 a.m. to 5 a.m.

The sales staff offers local sponsors the opportunity to air commercials or to sponsor segments within local broadcasts. They also negotiate barters, trading airtime for goods, like new cars for photographers or a wardrobe for

Visit Vault at **www.vault.com** for insider company profiles, expert advice, career message boards, expert resume reviews, the Vault Job Board and more.

VAULT CAREER LIBRARY   63

on-air talent. There are also sales reps at the local level who sell spots to national advertisers.

Following is the basic track for a sales career in broadcast television:

- Sales Assistant (Median entry-level salary is $20,000)
- Account Executive (local or national)
- Sales Manager
- General Sales Manager
- Vice President

Marketing & promotion: Promos, teases, interstitials and the overall brand image of a station falls under the domain of marketing in television news. New technologies are making producing promotional elements easier and easier, as well as cutting costs dramatically.

The promotions staff is responsible for the overall brand image of the station or news organization, as well as the marketing of each show and their individual segments. At some stations, producers are assuming more and more promotional responsibilities.

Below are some terms unique to promotions:

Promos: Basically commercials for upcoming stories or newscasts that may be of interest to viewers. The logic has always been that the best place to market television is on television itself, where the target audience is already watching.

Teases: Cleverly written introductions to a newscast. They are also used just before a commercial to entice the audience to keep watching.

Interstitials: Station identification spots or public service announcements that may or may not feature talent from the station.

Following is the basic track for a marketing career in broadcast television:

- Promotions Assistant (Median entry-level salary is $20,000)
- Promotions Producer
- Promotions Manager
- Creative Director
- Vice President

INSIGHTS FROM INDUSTRY LEADERS

Harry Smith
Anchor, CBS Early Show

In the fall of 2002, Smith returned to morning television when he was named anchor of *The Early Show* on CBS. He also continues to serve as the anchor of A&E's *Biography*. Smith has covered a wide range of stories, including the Second Gulf War, the First Gulf War, the 1996 Democratic and Republican National Conventions, the Oklahoma City Bombing and the Winter Olympics in Albertville, France and Lillehammer, Norway. He was also a regular contributor to the *CBS Evening News*, sharing stories from off the beaten path with his "Travels with Harry" segment. From 1987 to 1996, he served as co-anchor of *CBS This Morning*.

Q: What is the key to a successful career in television news?
A: Beyond having some brains and some talent, the three other major factors are determination, hard work and some luck. A lot of times hard work is maybe the most important factor. A lot of times people get to a certain level and think, "Geez, I've achieved x, y, or z..." One of the things I've realized is that you're entitled to nothing because you've made it to some certain level. That doesn't entitle you to anything. You just have to work that much harder to stay there.

Q: What are the ingredients to becoming a good storyteller?
A: Listening is the key thing. When Howard Stringer hired me to work at CBS, I did not have a vast amount of hard news experience. He thought I could write and that I was a decent enough storyteller. There's a certain amount of talent and there's a craft that you can develop, but the key is being able to listen. It's in the nuance. People will tell you a lot of things during an interview, but it's the things they tell you when they're not on camera; their attitudes and everything else. That all ends up playing a huge part in how you tell their story. Empathy is also important. Even if it's only for a moment, try to feel what it's like to be in your subject's shoes. Those are the two real keys to storytelling.

Q: What is the strength of television news in a media landscape of unlimited choices?
A: There are still millions of people who get their news from the three main networks; many more than get their news from any of the cable networks or all of them combined for that matter. I think the advantage of the digital world is that I have my choice of half a dozen different news sources all over the planet. As citizens, it behooves us to seek out as many points of view and different kinds of information as possible. I think it certainly challenges the old world of network news, but millions and millions of people still choose to get their news the old-fashioned way, and I think that leaves us with a pretty significant responsibility.

Q: How important is it for journalists to be up on their current events and to stay informed on as many issues as possible?
A: I work on a show with four anchors, and on any given day I may have one hard news segment to do, maybe two and sometimes three. I'm here every morning between 4 and 5 am. I pore through an entire stack of newspapers because you need to be prepared.

Case in point: Dan Rather was in Iraq during the handover, when the Iraqis regained their sovereignty, which was also the same time Saddam Hussein was being arraigned. Dan was over there live, and we went on the air without notes, without any text, and nobody had anything written down. He and I had to do several hours on the air with what was in our heads. Nobody was handing us note cards or wire stories. It came from what we'd learned reading all those papers every morning. That's the best part of this business – when they tell you Baghdad's on the line and we're going live with a special report in two minutes, so let's go. There's no safety net, it's all about you and what you know.

Visit Vault at **www.vault.com** for insider company profiles, expert advice, career message boards, expert resume reviews, the Vault Job Board and more.

VAULT CAREER LIBRARY

65

Network/Cable News Track

Producing

Production Assistant: An entry-level position performing administrative duties that vary from company to company and even from show to show.

Median Salary: $20,000

Broadcast Associate: In charge of gathering basic elements for a broadcast, including archival footage and research for producers.

Median Salary: $25,000

Booker: Focused on booking guests to be interviewed for live broadcasts. This position is common in cable news, as well as morning broadcasts that have a lot of live guests.

Median Salary: $40,000

Assistant or Associate Producer: Depending on the size of the organization, an assistant producer is junior to an associate producer, but they both perform similar functions. Responsibilities include setting up interviews, research, arranging and sometimes supervising shoots and gathering other elements required for a piece.

Median Salary: $45,000

Segment Producer: In charge of one portion of a broadcast, generally in between two blocks of commercials.

Median Salary: $45,000

Web Producer: An increasingly important part of each broadcast and news organization, overseeing the production of various web pages dedicated to a particular show or a specific topic area.

Median Salary: $30,000

Show Producer: Performs similar functions as a producer at the local level. Show producers generally work in cable news and oversee the rundown, script and elements for a show.

Median Salary: $50,000

Field Producer or Producer: Oversees the logistics of producing a story or elements for a piece in the field. After seeking approval of the executive producer for a story, they oversee its entire process, from developing an outline to identifying interview subjects to setting up interviews for correspondents; many times they even conduct the interviews themselves.

Median Salary: $60,000

Senior Producer: Works with producers to develop story ideas and to provide editorial guidance and suggestions.

Executive Producer: Oversees an entire broadcast. Responsibilities include setting budgets, helping to arrange high-profile interviews, developing story ideas and providing overall editorial direction for the broadcast.

National or Foreign Editor: Function is similar to that of an assignment editor. Keeps an eye on developing stories on national or international scene. Also coordinates the necessary resources for the coverage of domestic or foreign news events.

Senior Executive Producer: Within large news organizations, a Senior Executive Producer manages the overall brand of a show, particularly when there are multiple broadcasts under the same name, like *60 Minutes* or *Dateline*. Determines potential revenue opportunities, provides editorial guidance and steers the overall promotion of the broadcast.

Vice President: Oversees a specific operational area, like newsgathering, or a daypart, like primetime broadcasts.

President: Head of the news operation, providing overall editorial, financial and brand direction for organization.

On air

Correspondent: Functions much the same as reporters do at the local level, but they have a producer assigned to them, helping them put their video package together. They will write the script, but the producer gathers the elements. In cable news, they will also perform several live shots throughout the progression of a developing story.

For magazine shows or "soft news," correspondents conduct interviews and write the script for their piece. Stories for magazine shows can run as long as ten minutes, while packages for a hard news broadcast, like the evening news, run only about one and a half minutes.

Median Salary: $125,000

Visit Vault at **www.vault.com** for insider company profiles, expert advice, career message boards, expert resume reviews, the Vault Job Board and more.

VAULT CAREER LIBRARY   **67**

Anchor: As with local broadcasts, the anchor is the central figure of a show, introducing all the stories and correspondents. They will also conduct interviews on the set and sometimes in the field.

Salary: Varies, depending on the reach of the broadcast.

Local Television News Track

Assignment desk

Desk Assistant: An entry-level position at a local station on the assignment desk. Works with assignment editor to answer phones, read the wires, listen to the police and fire department scanners, as well as help coordinate photographers and reporters in the field.

Median Salary: $20,000

Assignment Editor: Manages the assignment desk. Generally there is a dayside assignment editor and a nightside assignment editor. Many stations also have an assignment editor to cover the overnight hours and to help prepare for the early morning newscasts. They pitch story ideas, assign reporters and photographers to stories and gather research to help with the development of stories.

Median Salary: $30,000

Producing

Production Assistant: Another entry-level position to help with administrative tasks and to provide additional support to the assignment desk, reporters, producers, photographers and editors.

Median Salary: $20,000

Associate Producer: After a year or so spent in an entry-level position, this is the next step on the road to becoming a producer. Works with producer(s) on one or two assigned newscasts, the 5 p.m. and 6 p.m. news, for example. Asked to write "readers," copy read by the anchor with no video, as well as introductions for reporter packages. May also edit video on a nonlinear editing system.

Median Salary: $22,000

Producer: Generally oversees one broadcast, sometimes two. Develops the "rundown," a document that determines the order of the stories in the newscasts and makes sure the entire newscast runs on time. Writes the opening headlines and some readers. Constantly monitors wires and assignment desk for breaking news, as well as the latest developments for existing stories.

Median Salary: $26,000

Executive Producer: Oversees all newscasts. Depending on the market, there may also be a Senior Producer who works with the Executive Producer. Works to make sure lead story is consistent throughout all newscasts. Works with producers to maintain editorial and production standards, as articulated by the station.

Median Salary: $49,000

Assistant News Director: Works with news director to manage entire newsgathering and production operation.

Median Salary: $55,000

News Director: Oversees all aspects of news gathering operation, from editorial to production to graphics, making sure the look and feel of all newscasts is consistent with the editorial standards and overall vision of the station.

Median Salary: $65,000

Photographer: The actual collection of video is gathered by photographers, or "photogs." Many photographers learn their trade on the job or receive Special training at a trade school. Like on-air talent and producers, they also move around the country to build their career.

Increasingly, more and more photogs are also wearing the editor's hat, due to shrinking budgets and new technologies that make it even easier to edit. Most photogs at local stations already edit a reporter's package, either back at the station or in a live truck (a vehicle used to broadcast from remote locations).

Median Salary: $24,000

On air

The "face" of the newsgathering operation is the reporters and anchors of each station, also referred to as "the talent." Becoming an on-air reporter or anchor is very tough. Most people will start out as a general assignment

Visit Vault at www.vault.com for insider company profiles, expert advice, career message boards, expert resume reviews, the Vault Job Board and more.

VAULT CAREER LIBRARY

69

reporter in a very small market and will move around the country every one to two years, jumping to larger markets with better financial compensation.

Some will also have to work less coveted schedules like overnights and weekends just to start building their career and demo tape. It is no longer uncommon for reporters to start out as "video journalists" or VJs. These reporters are virtual one-man bands. They use digital video cameras and laptop editing software, shooting and editing their own video, in addition to producing and writing their own story.

Median Salary for Reporters: $26,000

Median Salary for Anchors: $48,000

Meteorologist or Weatherman: Meteorologists possess a degree in meteorology or atmospheric science, whereas some weathermen do not. Much of today's weather forecasting is left to high-powered computers that offer various models to predict the weather. Weather is one of the most popular segments of local broadcasts. There are both on-air and producing opportunities in weather. Beyond television stations, there are also opportunities on cable at The Weather Channel and local 24/7 weather channels, as well as weather service companies like AccuWeather or WeatherCentral.

Sportscaster or Sports Anchor: In some cases, a station's lead sports anchor is also referred to as the sports director. There is a growing emphasis within some local television stations on reducing their sports staff and delegating coverage of sports to the news staff, as a result of increasing competition from sports cable networks and web sites. Alternatively, there are more and more opportunities to work in sports cable television, as well as for professional sports organizations and leagues that have recently launched their own networks.

Understanding the Industry

Current trends

Fragmentation of the Audience: In the early 1980s, the three major broadcast networks, CBS, NBC and ABC, commanded over 80 percent of the market share. Since then, Fox has joined their ranks as the fourth major broadcast network, and their combined audience has shrunk to less than 50 percent. Broadcast television now competes with cable, satellite TV, the

Internet, video games and seemingly unlimited media choices. Some senior broadcast television executives now see the competition for the consumer's time as the greatest threat to their business, which has been based on delivering the largest audience possible to advertisers.

Workflow Consolidation: The various roles in television news are now beginning to blur, as a result of cheaper and easier to use technologies like digital video cameras and laptop editing systems. Broadcast technicians and editors have been impacted most severely. Most studio cameras are now robotic, and many stations are now automating their production system. Producers and reporters are increasingly taking over basic editing functions using nonlinear editing systems. Within organizations like Time Warner's NY1 in New York, reporters do it all, from setting up their own stories to shooting and editing their own video to even operating the camera for their own live shots.

Digital Television: The television industry has been mandated by the government to switch from their analog signal to their digital one by 2009. The conversion to digital is opening up a variety of new opportunities for both broadcast and cable television. It will now be possible for broadcasters to have multiple digital channels. Some local markets have already started airing their own local 24/7 news and/or weather channels.

Industry Snapshot

Overall Value of Broadcast TV: $40 billion

Overall Value of Cable & Satellite TV: $83 billion

Number Employed by Broadcast TV: 127,000

Ad Spending Growth for 2003: .5%

Total Number of Stations: 1,700

Top 5 Markets: New York, Los Angeles, Chicago, Philadelphia, San Francisco

Visit Vault at **www.vault.com** for insider company profiles, expert advice, career message boards, expert resume reviews, the Vault Job Board and more.

VAULT CAREER LIBRARY

71

Breaking Down Television News

Local Television News: The United States is broken up into different "designated market areas," or DMAs, based on population and wealth. Today there are 210 DMAs. New York is number one, while Glendive, MT is 210. These communities are served by stations affiliated with major networks like NBC, CBS, ABC and Fox or are independent. Smaller communities generally have fewer stations compared with those in the top 10 markets, which may have as many as 10 stations.

Over the last decade, Spanish-language broadcasters Univision and Telemundo have been aggressively building affiliate stations, particularly in markets with large Latino populations like California, the Southwest and Florida.

Affiliate stations fill their airtime with programming from their network, buy the rights to syndicated programming and also produce local news programming. On average, those stations that produce local news broadcast from 5 a.m. to 7 a.m., at noon, from 5 p.m. to 6:30 p.m. and at 11 p.m. Some stations don't produce any local news, while others are producing more and more of it. Local news programming is the primary revenue driver for most stations, as well as the only opportunity to brand the station within the local community it serves.

Network News: Despite the proliferation of cable news channels, most Americans still get their news from network news divisions. On average, over 25 million people watch one of the three major evening news broadcasts, compared with the 2 million people who watch *The O'Reilly Factor* on the Fox News Channel, one of the most popular programs in cable news.

Network news programming falls into two categories, "hard news" and "soft news." Evening news broadcasts, special events like the Presidential election coverage, and breaking news fall under hard news. Technically, morning shows like *Today* and *Good Morning America* are considered hard news, but with the majority of those broadcasts now filled with soft fare like cooking segments and weight loss stories, that designation is a stretch. News magazines like *48 Hours* or *Dateline* fall under soft news or lifestyle-oriented stories.

Cable News: Network news divisions have increasingly turned to soft news because they have found it challenging to compete with the 24/7 newsgathering operations of CNN and Fox News. MSNBC is a partnership between NBC News and Microsoft. While MSNBC is third amongst the major cable news channels, it has provided NBC with the economic advantage of using one newsgathering operation to air content on two networks. CNBC also falls into cable news, but is focused on business news. During the late 1990s, it saw its ratings explode before the bubble burst, but has now shifted from hard economic news to more business lifestyle news.

Over the last few years, cable operations are turning to more magazine shows, as the networks have, in an effort to create more appointment viewing. The result has been a litany of talking heads and opinion-based programming, from Bill O'Reilly to Anderson Cooper to former heavy hitters like Phil Donohue and Connie Chung, who have yet to reclaim their former glory.

Public Television: In 1960, the federal government established the Corporation for Public Broadcasting, founding PBS as part of this initiative. PBS is supported by government funds, donations from viewers, and is underwritten by corporations. Some of the most well known PBS news and information programs include *The News Hour with Jim Lehrer, Nova* and *Frontline*. Unlike broadcast networks, PBS is a loose association of local affiliates that operate with a high degree of independence and control most of their local programming. Much of the programming on PBS stations is locally produced, bought from production companies or from other PBS stations.

Key Players

National broadcast & cable networks

ABC News
77 West 66th St.
New York, NY 10023
Phone: 212-456-6200
Web: www.abcnews.com

CBS News
524 West 57th St.
New York, NY 10019
Phone: 212-975-4321
Web: www.cbsnews.com

Visit Vault at **www.vault.com** for insider company profiles, expert advice, career message boards, expert resume reviews, the Vault Job Board and more.

VAULT CAREER LIBRARY   73

CNBC

1 CNBC Plaza
Englewood Cliffs, NJ 07632
Phone: 201-735-2622
Web: moneycentral.msn.com

CNN

1 CNN Center
Atlanta, GA 30303
Phone: 404-827-1500
Web: www.cnn.com

Fox News Channel

1211 Avenue of the Americas
New York, NY 10036
Phone: 212-301-3000
Web: www.foxnews.com

MSNBC

1 MSNBC Plaza
Secaucus, NJ 07094
Phone: 201-583-5000
Web: www.msnbc.com

NBC News

30 Rockefeller Plaza
New York, NY 10112
Phone: 212-664-4444
Web: www.msnbc.com

PBS

1320 Braddock Pl
Alexandria, VA 22314-1692
Phone: 703-739-5000
Web: www.pbs.org

The Weather Channel

300 Interstate North Parkway
Atlanta, GA 30339
Phone: 770-226-2609
Web: www.weather.com

74 © 2005 Vault Inc.

Visit TVSpy at www.tvspy.com for the TVSpy Job Bank, free industry newsletters,
insider message boards and other television career resources.

Local television

ABC Television Stations
500 South Buena Vista St.
Burbank, CA 91521-4472
Phone: 818-460-5600

BELO Corp.
400 South Record St.
Dallas, TX 75202
Phone: 214-977-6606
Web: www.belo.com

Clear Channel Television
200 East Basse Rd.
San Antonio, TX 78209
Phone: 210-822-2828
Web: www.clearchannel.com

Cox Television
6205 Peachtree Dunwoody Rd.
Atlanta, GA 30328
Phone: 678-645-0000
Web: www.coxenterprises.com

Emmis Communications
One Emmis Plaza
40 Monument Circle, Suite 700
Indianapolis, IN 46204
Phone: 317-266-0100
Web: www.emmis.com

Fisher Communications
600 University St., Suite 1525
Seattle, WA 98101
Phone: 206-404-7000
Web: www.fsci.com

Fox Television Stations
1999 South Bundy Dr.
Los Angeles, CA 90025-5235
Phone: 310-584-2000
Web: www.newscorp.com

Visit Vault at **www.vault.com** for insider company profiles, expert advice,
career message boards, expert resume reviews, the Vault Job Board and more.

VAULT CAREER LIBRARY   75

Freedom Broadcasting
17666 Fitch
Irvine, CA 92614-6022
Phone: 949-253-2315
Web: www.freedom.com

Gannett Broadcasting
7950 Jones Branch Dr.
McLean, VA 22107
Phone: 703-854-6000
Web: www.gannett.com

Granite Broadcasting
767 Third Ave.
New York, NY 10017
Phone: 212-826-2530
Web: www.granitetv.com

Gray MidAmerica Television
126 N. Washington St.
Albany, GA 31701
Phone: 229-888-9390
Web: www.graycommunications.com

Hearst-Argyle Television
888 Seventh Ave., 27th Floor
New York, NY 10106
Phone: 212-887-6800
Web: www.hearstargyle.com

Liberty Corporation
P.O. Box 502
Greenville, SC 29602
Phone: 864-241-5400
Web: www.libertycorp.com

LIN TV Corp.
4 Richmond Square #200
Providence, RI 02906
Phone: 401-454-2880
Web: www.lintv.com

Media General Broadcast Group
111 North 4th St.
Richmond, VA 23219
Phone: 804-775-4600
Web: www.mgbg.com

Meredith Corporation
1716 Locust St.
Des Moines, IA 50309
Phone: 515-284-3696
Web: www.meredith.com

NBC Universal Television
30 Rockefeller Plaza
New York, NY 10112
Phone: 212-664-4444
Web: www.nbc.com

New York Times Broadcast Group
803 Channel 3 Dr.
Memphis, TN 38103
Phone: 901-543-2333

Nexstar Broadcasting Group
909 Lake Carolyn Parkway, Suite 1450
Irving, TX 75039
Phone: 972-373-8800
Web: www.nexstarbroadcasting.com

Pappas Telecasting Companies
500 South Chinowth Rd.
Visalia, CA 93277-1617
Phone: 559-733-7800
Web: www.pappastv.com

Pegasus Broadcast Television
225 City Line Ave., Suite 200
Bala Cynwyd, PA 19004
Phone: 610-934-7052
Web: www.pgtv.com

Visit Vault at **www.vault.com** for insider company profiles, expert advice,
career message boards, expert resume reviews, the Vault Job Board and more.

VAULT CAREER LIBRARY   77

Piedmont Television
7621 Little Ave., Suite 506
Charlotte, NC 28226
Phone: 704-341-0944
Web: www.piedmonttv.com

Post-Newsweek Stations
550 West Lafayette Blvd.
Detroit, MI 48226
Phone: 313-223-2260

Raycom Media
201 Monroe St. RSA Tower, 20th Floor
Montgomery, AL 36104
Phone: 334-206-1400
Web: www.raycommedia.com

Scripps Howard Broadcasting
P.O. Box 5380
Cincinnati, OH 45201
Phone: 513-977-3000
Web: www.scripps.com

Sinclair Broadcast Group
10706 Beaver Dam Rd.
Hunt Valley, MD 21030
Phone: 410-568-1500
Web: www.sbgi.net

Tribune Broadcasting
435 North Michigan Ave., 18th Floor
Chicago, IL 60611
Phone: 312-222-3333
Web: www.tribune.com

Viacom Television Stations Group
Columbia Square 6121 Sunset Blvd.
Los Angeles, CA 90028
Phone: 323-460-3459
Web: www.viacom.com

Young Broadcasting
599 Lexington Ave., 47th Floor
New York, NY 10022
Phone: 212-754-7070
Web: www.youngbroadcasting.com

Visit Vault at **www.vault.com** for insider company profiles, expert advice,
career message boards, expert resume reviews, the Vault Job Board and more.

V∧ULT CAREER LIBRARY

79

INNOVATIVE SOLUTIONS

Will J. Wright

General Manager, HDNews

Building a Newscast as Unique as Its Technology: Overcoming Basic Problems of HD

Challenge

RTNDA/NAB 2004 was a coming out party for Rainbow Media's HDNews, the nation's first 24/7 national newscast, broadcast via satellite entirely in native high definition. HDNews was at RTNDA to spread the gospel of HD and to enlist support from fellow broadcasters as the U.S. strives to catch up with Europe and Japan in broadcasting in high definition.

At the RTNDA Convention, we demonstrated HDNews to a number of vendors who were interested in providing us with syndicated packages of various genres. They, along with everyone else who watched our news, were impressed with the 16x9 aspect ratio, the picture clarity and the color brilliance. But there was an "intangible" quality that presented a challenge to anyone hoping to sell us material to put on our air. That intangible was the fact that while the audio was turned down, and sometimes totally drowned out by the noise in the hall, the context and meaning of our stories beamed through with remarkable silent coherence. The video and juxtaposition of the pictures spoke volumes, which was tribute to the photographers, editors and reporters who are providing us with this remarkable material.

Strategies & Solutions

We seized an opportunity to continue to do what is not now being done on a routine basis on any news channel – to codify a unique storytelling style. And what's really nice about this opportunity is that our style has already emerged. The HDNews style can be attributed to the understanding by everyone involved in this project that native "hi def" means applying a higher definition to everything we do for this news channel as we continue to build this extraordinary product from the ground up.

It is important that we first grasp the concept of why we exist as a news channel. We are a "destination interstitial" for VOOM subscribers. When most people buy our VOOM Originals package, they understand that they will be getting entertainment, music and sports. What surprises them and most people who preview our VOOM Originals package is that news is being offered, and it is not an up-converted version of what can be found anywhere else. And therein lies the sparkle and magic that our product exhibited on the floor of RTNDA.

Consider yourself an observer watching traffic and describing what is going on from a ninth-story window above the street. You could very well paint a picture with the visual information available to you, but imagine if you were down on the street standing right on the yellow line. Well, that's where we are compared to everyone else doing news today. We're on the yellow line. And the opportunity to do "dramatically visual storytelling" presents itself to us every time we do a package.

Results

The observer on the ninth floor can only describe to the viewer what is going on and has to use a lot more words to render details to the story. In our visual storytelling style, the viewer becomes the observer and the people whom the story is about tell the story.

The news set, created in collaboration with celebrated set designer Tim Hunter, was designed with HD in mind. The colors, textures and materials are seen nowhere else on an American set, done by custom wood and metal workers at the cost of a small house. Our graphics package was created by Pyburn Films, a team headed by the super-creative Randy Pyburn, who won the contract over five other graphics houses by submitting a uniquely dramatic graphics package that exploited the 16x9 aspect ratio and with music that takes advantage of the drama that can be created by a hi def picture.

Our editors learned how to extract Dolby 5.1 and send sound all around the room, so as you watch VOOM HDNews at home you are totally immersed in the viewing experience. With the technical aspects in check, attention turned to content, and delivering what is not being done elsewhere.

We realize that we are way ahead of the curve and are taking steps to create alliances with news organizations, individuals and technology providers to bring US television into this new technology. When you look around and consider our position in technical dominance, high def is the new battleground, and HDNews is the leading edge of this new wave.

Visit Vault at **www.vault.com** for insider company profiles, expert advice, career message boards, expert resume reviews, the Vault Job Board and more.

VAULT CAREER LIBRARY   81

The Inside Scoop

Must read

ShopTalk: A free daily newsletter covering broadcast and cable television news.
www.tvspy.com

TVWeek: A weekly print trade magazine dedicated to covering all aspects of the television industry.
www.tvweek.com

Broadcasting & Cable: A weekly print trade magazine focused on broadcast and cable television.
www.broadcastingcable.com

Variety: Trade magazine covering Hollywood and related entertainment industries.
www.variety.com

Speak the language

B-Roll: Various different shots of the same subject using different angles. Footage is generally used for VOs, SOT, readers and in packages.

Block: Any segment of a newscast. Includes everything between the commercials.

Cold Open: Technique to begin broadcast by jumping right into a story, rather than using an established introduction with graphics and music.

Designated Market Area (DMA): A geographic designation, used by Nielsen, that specifies which counties fall into a specific television market.

Franchise: A regularly broadcast segment focused on a particular topic or content area that is a "sub-brand" of the newscast and/or local station.

Kicker: The light-hearted story that ends a newscast.

Landscape or Establishing Shot: Video of the exteriors of an event location, such as a crime scene.

Natural Sound (NatSnd): The sounds recorded at the scene – wind blowing, engines running or crowd noise that was a natural part of the location.

Package: A reporter's story told on tape, with video clips of people he or she has interviewed, plus animation, graphics, stills or other visual elements.

Rating: The estimate of the size of a television audience relative to the total television households (108 million in the U.S.), expressed as a percentage.

Reader: Story read by the anchor, without any video.

Script: All copy read by anchor(s) throughout the newscast as indicated by the rundown, the outline of the newscast.

Share: The percent of the Households Using Television (HUT), which are tuned to a specific program or station at a specified time.

Sound on Tape (SOT): Reporter does a voice-on-tape lead in to a sound bite, then back to the live shot. Also may be a package with no live shot or standup introduced by anchor.

Soundbite: Quote from an interview subject on video.

Standup: Reporter recorded on tape, sharing information about a story between two other pieces of video and/or soundbites.

Sticks: Tripod for a camera.

Sweeps (the book): Period during which Nielsen ratings are measured to determine the size of the audience each television show draws. The television season starts in the fall and ends in the spring, so the sweeps periods are held during November, February, May and July.

Tease: Copy read by the anchor, promoting upcoming stories just before the commercial break, to entice viewers to stay tuned to hear the full story.

Voice Over (VO): Video with anchor or reporter reading over the pictures.

White Balance: A camera function which gives a reference to "true white," in order for the camera to interpret all colors correctly. Generally, a cameraperson will focus on a white sheet of paper as a reference point.

Join the club

American Federation of Television and Radio Artists
Phone: 212-532-0800
Web: www.aftra.org

Visit Vault at **www.vault.com** for insider company profiles, expert advice,
career message boards, expert resume reviews, the Vault Job Board and more.

VAULT CAREER LIBRARY   **83**

American Women in Radio and Television (AWRT)
Phone: 703-506-3290
Web: www.awrt.org

Best Practices in Journalism
Phone: 608-265-8071
Web: www.bpjtv.org

Center for Communications
Phone: 212-686-5005
Web: www.cencom.org

National Association of Broadcasters
Phone: 202-429-5300
Web: www.nab.org

NewsLab
Phone: 301-652-4881
Web: www.newslab.org

Poynter Institute
Phone: 888-769-6837
Web: www.poynter.org

Radio and Television News Directors Association
Phone: 202-659-6510
Web: www.rtnda.org

Job leads

NAB Job Bank
www.nab.org

RTNDA Job Bank
www.rtnda.org

TVJobs
www.tvjobs.com

TVSpy Job Bank
www.tvspy.com

Keep Your Career Moving Forward

Special training

By far the best way to break into television news is through internships. They enable you to understand the inner workings of broadcast television, build contacts and gain experience. If you have the opportunity to do more than one internship, do it. Try to land an internship at both a local station and a national news organization. Many news operations like CNN, CBS News and NBC News have special summer internship programs.

As with other media, a journalism degree will enhance your resume, but won't necessarily land you a job. Television is undergoing a radical technological transformation from analog to digital. This process will level the playing field dramatically, and lower the barriers to entry for people seeking to build video media organizations.

If you have access to a digital video camera and a laptop editing system like Final Cut Pro, start learning how to shoot and edit your own video. In larger cities like New York, Los Angeles, Boston, Chicago and Houston, there are now emerging workshops and schools that are training people to become "video journalists." Like it or not, your first job will be at a station in a small market where you will most likely have to do everything.

Landing your first job

Many of the entry-level jobs once used to launch careers in television are disappearing, due to technological changes, budget cuts and consolidation. Management is more eager to hire young broadcast journalists, however, because they will generally work for less and hold fewer prejudices than their elder counterparts.

The road to TV is through the web: Yes, you may want to pursue a career in broadcast journalism, but a new way to enter the business is through the web sites of broadcast news organizations. Many broadcasters are coming to realize that the Internet isn't going anywhere and that they need to start investing in their web properties if they want remain competitive in the future. You will also have far more creative opportunities working on the web, rather than being confined to the formulaic structure of television news.

For those interested in sales, learn how to sell for the web. It is a very different medium than television, and almost no one in broadcasting understands how to

Visit Vault at **www.vault.com** for insider company profiles, expert advice, career message boards, expert resume reviews, the Vault Job Board and more.

VAULT CAREER LIBRARY   85

sell advertising on the web. It's a wide-open field. Become a web sales expert in broadcasting – they need you desperately!

Embrace video journalism: Again, learning how to shoot with a digital video camera and editing on a nonlinear editing system are virtually becoming required skills for anyone seeking to enter the business for the first time. Budgets are tight. If you don't have a journalism degree, but know how to shoot and edit, you will be hired over anyone with a journalism degree and no technical experience.

Start small: This is true for both production and sales – start out in a smaller operation or market. You will be given far greater responsibility, gain experience more quickly, and it's always better to make your mistakes in Nowheresville, USA than in New York or Los Angeles.

Demo tapes: Going through a journalism program or attending a broadcast school does give aspiring on-air talent the opportunity to build a demo tape for their job hunt. If you are really nice to one of the photographers at your internships, they can also help you put something together.

A word on agents: If you are just starting out, you really don't need an agent. Quite honestly, the percentage they take from your salary isn't worth it to them compared with landing a contract for someone who has an established name. Pounding the pavement on your own will get you much further in most cases, and you'll get to keep your entire salary!

Getting your career unstuck

During the first three or four years of your career, keep moving around. It is not uncommon for people to change jobs once a year when they are starting out. You will boost your salary, give yourself a promotion, gain experience and make more contacts. Promotions are becoming a rarity in broadcasting. When they do come, they are often awarded as a result of frustrated employees' threats to leave, and still offer very little in the way of a raise.

Many television journalists build their careers, and their salaries, by criss-crossing the country, jumping to larger and larger markets. Some find living all over the country a rewarding experience, while others find it to be an unfulfilling and lonely existence. Staying in the same market may not boost your salary, but your quality of life will be greater than the life of a nomad. It is up to you to weigh the tradeoffs.

By the time television journalists reach their thirties, they either begin to enter management roles or decide to exit the industry. Some who leave television feel burned out after years of working odd hours and keeping a demanding schedule. A common exit strategy is to switch over to public relations, where journalists can put their skills to use in a related field that offers a much more stable and predictable lifestyle.

Documentaries

Defining exactly what a documentary is has always been elusive. The earliest "moving pictures" were by definition documentaries. They were generally non-fiction films or cinematic expressions meant to be factual. Documentaries can be further defined as the recording of events, using film or video, set to a narrative that may take a more objective journalistic tone or one that may promote a certain set of opinions.

In its broadest form, documentary now includes news, informational broadcasts, reality programs and instructional videos. Most people think of a documentary as an obscure film based on facts shown at a local art house or on PBS. Over the last decade however, the documentary format has exploded and taken on new forms, such as the proliferation of newsmagazines, as well as "real life" and "how to" programs on cable television.

What makes documentaries unique?

Documentaries have the broadest canvas in electronic journalism on which to tell a story. On some levels, they can also be regarded as the video version of magazines, although they go much deeper than what is termed a "newsmagazine" on broadcast television. They enable the viewer to immerse themselves in a very specific story. A documentary may last a half hour, one hour, or may be aired over several episodes as a series. Most other journalistic disciplines are focused on reporting current news and events, whereas documentaries delve into the past or into the most granular levels of a current issue. Documentaries also offer multiple angles of the same story, so as to provide a more layered picture of an event.

As of late, the documentary format is becoming increasingly elastic. Traditional documentaries maintain journalistic standards, attempting to provide an objective view of a historical or current event. Documentaries like *Fahrenheit 9/11* or *Outfoxed* have bent the rules to push a partisan agenda. Some reality programs have also absorbed elements of the documentary style of storytelling. It can be argued that the first *Real World* on MTV displayed many of the tenets of documentaries, witnessing the life of a diverse group of young adults living in New York. But as the wave of reality programs has washed over the landscape of television, many of them have become heavily scripted and have little similarity to the basic documentary style.

What attracts people to work in documentaries?

There are two reasons people become involved with documentary filmmaking. Some are attracted to the aesthetics and longer format of documentaries, and others are more interested in the capacity of documentaries to promote or maximize interest in certain social issues. Unlike a newspaper or television reporter who is driven by the immediacy of news, documentary producers and filmmakers relish the opportunity to steep themselves in one story that may take months or years to produce.

Is a Career in Documentaries for You?

Lifestyle

If working 9 to 5, Monday through Friday, is not your thing, then documentary filmmaking may offer the freedom you are seeking in your work. However, you will be working more than 40 hours a week more often than not (when you have work), and the only thing consistent about your schedule is that it will never be regular. Most of your work will be on a project-by-project basis, so you may find yourself busier at times than others.

If you choose to be an independent producer or a freelancer, it is wise to consider a course in personal finance to help you learn how to manage both your personal and professional budgets. You can also seek the advice of an accountant or your bank.

Desired skills & traits

Entrepreneurship: Far and away the most important trait necessary to become a successful documentary filmmaker. It will take an immense amount of faith, persistence and yes, a little luck, to endure the low pay, long hours, rejection and the normal headaches of production. If that doesn't deter you, then you have a fighting chance.

Storytelling: Whether it's a documentary about nature, a historical re-enactment or a reality-based film, you have to have a clear point for your narrative, pulling the viewer in and guiding them through the beginning, middle and end of a story. If you are lucky, the subject of your film will leave a deep impression on your audience.

Organizational Skills: An important skill when you are starting out as a production assistant. Make lots of lists and create a simple "database," using an Excel spreadsheet, to keep track of schedules, contact information and your litany of "to do" lists.

Salary Expectations

There are a variety of different variables that influence compensation in documentary filmmaking. Rates vary from project to project and company to company. If you are seeking a job at a production company, it is best to ask people working in production in the same city what the going wage is. If you are pitching a project, your rate will depend on how much money the network or distribution channel has to spend on new programming. It also depends on the potential size of the audience and level of interest expressed by sponsors in the project.

Career Track

Key positions at a production company

Production Assistant: As with other entry-level roles, PAs are basically gofers and provide administrative support where needed.

Writer: May write the original script or provide edits to one that has already been written. During shooting and production, the writer is available to rewrite certain passages as circumstances call for them. The script is never final until the editing process has been completed.

Associate Producer: Provides assistance to the producer(s). May fill in for a producer when she or he isn't available. A line producer also assists a producer with budgeting, tracking and scheduling issues.

Producer: In charge of the "big picture" of the production. Producers are busy setting up for the next shoot while the director is overseeing the current one being shot. They are in charge of the budget, schedule, locations, crew and editorial inconsistencies.

Executive Producer: Oversees the entire production process and makes all key editorial, financial and production decisions.

Director: In charge of each scene shot, including the lighting, sound, composition, content and performance.

Directory of Photography: In lower-budget productions, also referred to as the photographer or cameraperson. Makes technical decisions about the movement and consistency of each shot.

Visit Vault at **www.vault.com** for insider company profiles, expert advice, career message boards, expert resume reviews, the Vault Job Board and more.

V∧ULT CAREER LIBRARY   **89**

INSIGHTS FROM INDUSTRY LEADERS

Michael Rosenblum

Founder, DVDojo

For well over a decade, Michael Rosenblum has been the leading advocate of the digital "video journalist" revolution. Some of his projects include the creation of "VJ" units at the BBC, the complete conversion of The Voice of America, the implementation of the VJ concept at Time Warner's NY1, and countless other broadcast operations across the globe. He is also founder and president of New York Times Television.

Rosenblum estimates that he has trained more than 3,000 journalists in his drive to help "democratize television." A few years ago, he founded DVDojo, a video journalism training school in New York, where anyone can learn how to make films, documentaries or television all on their own using DV cameras and nonlinear editing systems.

Q: You often used the phrase "freedom to fail." What do you mean by that?
A: That's a very important thing. In any creative endeavor, you have to be willing to honor failure. If you're a writer, every time you put a piece of paper in the typewriter and it doesn't come out right, you have to throw it out and try again. If every piece of paper cost you $1,000, you wouldn't do that. Digital video drives the costs of production so low that it allows people to take risks and fail without penalty. You can only do good journalism if you're able to take risks and fail occasionally.

Q: Traditional television producers may argue that you are killing the spirit of collaboration if one person's doing all the shooting, editing, and producing. How do you respond to that?
A: I don't want collaboration. When a print journalist goes out to cover a story, he or she doesn't have somebody else write it and somebody else type it. This notion of collaboration is a complete misnomer, and frankly, it dilutes the quality of the story. I'm looking for authorship, and authorship is an individual experience.

Q: What's your favorite documentary, and why?
A: It's tough to say. Each documentary tends to reflect the technical limitations of its time. When I went to school, they would always show *Harvest of Shame*. When you watch it now, you just cringe. What was cutting edge twenty years ago can now be an embarrassment, so I'm not sure there's anything from back then I can point to as an example of great documentary filmmaking.

Q: What common mistakes do people make when they set out to pursue a career in documentary filmmaking?
A: They tend to make the film before they've sold it to somebody. That's one of the big mistakes people make. You need to sell the concept first, then make the film.

Q: What is your vision for the media world?
A: I think we're going to see convergence between radio, television, and the Internet, although that's pretty obvious. I think that television in particular, and the way that it's made, will come to parallel the way print is made. Thousands of people at home, freelancing on their computers, will create their own content for a rather large, broad and variegated array of output. I think that's where the technology is taking us.

In another kind of convergence, the newsroom of the future will very much come to resemble the dot-com offices of the 1990s – hundreds of people at computers, only instead of web pages they'll be producing video. The technology has already converged.

The Making of a Documentary

The idea

As with everything else in life, all documentaries start as an idea. Most documentaries are inspired by political or social issues, history, or stories about the human spirit. As you consider a topic for your documentary, first consider your own personal sources of inspiration. Is it a person, specific event, cause, issue or a place? Generally when you write about something you already know a lot about, or are inspired by a special event or issue, your passion will shine through.

Once you have settled on your topic, it's time to develop a story. You should start by creating a "project treatment," a description and assessment of your goals for the project. You should consider your potential target audience, and how your film will be distributed. Knowing your audience will make your documentary even more effective. Develop a list of people you would want to interview, footage you need to acquire or shoot, and any other elements you think you will need to tell your story.

There are several different styles of documentary storytelling. Following are some different modes identified by Bill Nichols in 1991:

Poetic: Stresses the mood, tone, and affect much more than displays of knowledge or acts of persuasion. It also opens up the possibility of alternative forms of presentation of knowledge as opposed to the straightforward transfer of information.

Expository: The filmmaker presents events in a more rhetorical or argumentative frame.

Observational: The filmmaker simply observes what happens in front of the camera without overt intervention. S/he acts as a witness to history.

Participatory: The filmmaker lives among a group of people who are the subject of the documentary to gain a visceral feel for what life is like through their eyes.

Reflexive: The engagement is between the filmmaker and his or her audience, rather than between the filmmaker and his or her characters in the documentary. This style also deals with the problem of representing and portraying history in addition to the social or political points being presented in the film. It's not just about what gets represented, but how.

Visit Vault at **www.vault.com** for insider company profiles, expert advice, career message boards, expert resume reviews, the Vault Job Board and more.

VAULT CAREER LIBRARY

91

Performative: Like the poetic mode of documentary representation, the performative mode raises questions about what knowledge is. It considers other knowledge that helps in our understanding of the world beyond factual information alone.

Business plan & funding

A business plan demonstrating how your project can generate revenues is just as important as the script. Costs vary from project to project. Even if your project is on a shoestring budget, it is a good idea to get in the habit of putting together a basic budget, so you understand the costs involved. It is also important to understand the impact of time on those costs, the value of different audiences and the forms of distribution you may consider for your documentary. Yes, there is an audience for almost anything, but you may not want to keep making obscure documentaries that keep you on a diet of mac and cheese for the rest of your life.

Fortunately, new technologies like digital video cameras and laptop editing systems are dramatically cutting the costs of producing a documentary. If your documentary calls for a cinematographer, actors to portray reconstructed events, extensive travel, or rights to footage you do not own, these factors will significantly raise the cost of your production. As you seek funding for your documentary, think of yourself as a modern Renaissance artist looking for a wealthy patron. There is someone out there willing to take a chance on you, especially if they feel your passion. Funding can come from the most unlikely sources, so be creative.

Below are some sources of funding for your documentary:

Production Company: Most independent production companies have a development department that accept and review submissions for possible financial backing for your documentary. Many in the industry regard these departments as "black holes," particularly if you are an unknown producer. Owners of production companies generally consider pitches from known sources in the industry, but occasionally do take a chance on a dark horse.

Network or Cable Channel: PBS has a formal submission process whereby they may offer a grant to produce your documentary. They may also have you sign a pre-sale agreement, in which they buy your documentary before it is sold. Other cable networks, like Discovery or the Independent Film Channel, have similar arrangements.

Foundations and Grants: There are countless sources of grant money offered by federal, state and local governments, as well as universities and nonprofit organizations. Target organizations that you believe would have a vested interested in your documentary and how it may help advance their research or cause.

Sponsorships: Many corporations also have foundations, and may regard your documentary as the perfect sponsorship opportunity. If you bring a sponsor to the table, most distributors won't say no to your documentary.

Private Investors: With your idea and business plan in hand, ask for backing from your family, your parents' friends, and other potential contacts you believe could offer you financial support. Why not? As they say, charity begins at home!

Specialized Loans: Most likely a long shot, but it is possible that a bank or another source of private equity could extend you a loan, particularly if you have a business plan that demonstrates how your project will make money.

Distribution

Depending on your target audience or your source of funding, your documentary may be intended for a private or public audience. If you are distributing your documentary publicly, there are three primary means of distribution.

Television: Documentaries have been a huge source of programming for PBS through the years. As cable television has grown over the last two decades, networks like the Discovery Channel, The Learning Channel and A&E have become major distributors of documentary programs.

Theaters & Film Festivals: Film festivals are an important distribution channel that can help build buzz about your documentary. They are held all over the country, throughout the year. The two most prestigious are Sundance and Cannes. Festivals provide you with exposure and an opportunity to network, to build contacts for future funding and distribution if your documentary doesn't get picked up. If your documentary isn't bought outright, there is still the opportunity that it may be shown in selected theaters in larger cities to a more limited audience.

Direct Distribution: The emerging digital world now provides direct access for documentary producers to a worldwide audience via the Internet and DVDs. A recent documentary, *Outfoxed*, bypassed all traditional forms of distribution, sending DVDs through the U.S. Postal Service to people who

Visit Vault at **www.vault.com** for insider company profiles, expert advice, career message boards, expert resume reviews, the Vault Job Board and more.

VAULT CAREER LIBRARY   93

volunteered their homes for semi-public viewings. On July 18, 2004, an estimated 30,000 people saw the documentary.

While not a documentary, the phenomenon of Jibjab.com, in which cut-outs of George Bush and John Kerry sing a version of "This Land Is Your Land" using pot shots as the lyrics, may provide lessons on distributing film shorts online. The first day of its release, the web site crashed because it was flooded with visitors. It ended up attracting national attention for its creators, even landing them an interview on *The Today Show.*

Promotion

The marketing and promotions process really begins with the inception of your idea. Not only are you selling your documentary, you are selling yourself, as well as getting people excited about your idea. Think about who you have to "sell" your documentary to – financial backers, distributors and the target audience. Some will say all you need to focus on is making a great film, and word of mouth buzz will publicize your film for you. If you happen to win a prize at a film festival, there's no better way to build buzz for your film!

Producers with larger budgets will hire a publicist to handle all the marketing and public relations efforts for the documentary. For someone with a small budget, making posters, postcards and even a web site are effective ways to promote your documentary, particularly when you show it at a film festival. You should also have some VHS and DVD copies ready to hand out to people you meet at festivals.

Understanding the Industry

Current trends

Direct Distribution: Documentary filmmakers have traditionally been beholden to film festivals, local art houses and public television to get their work shown in public. The proliferation of cable channels over the last decade has spiked demand for documentary and reality programming. It is relatively cheap to produce, and the format can be used to target a wide variety of "under-served" audiences.

Broadband and DVDs are now opening up another channel of distribution, going directly to the people, circumventing traditional distribution like television or theaters. Producer Robert Greenwald teamed up with MoveOn.org, a political action group, to distribute his documentary Outfoxed to their members, who volunteered their homes as viewing sites. It was estimated that over 3,000 viewing parties were organized. Typically, many documentaries today focus on a specific topic and appeal to a niche audience, thus the opportunity to distribute them via the Internet or DVDs has been far from realized.

Shooting in HD: The rules of shooting in High Definition are now just being written. As consumers buy more and more HD television sets, the demand for HD programming will only grow. Much of the subject matter of documentaries, such as travel, science and nature, is perfectly suited for the crystal clear pictures of the HD experience. High def offers filmmakers a new canvas on which to express their vision.

Reality & Partisan Docs: The explosion of reality programming and films like *Fahrenheit 9/11* and *Super Size Me* are bringing the documentary format and elements of documentary filmmaking to a much wider audience than ever before. Political groups have embraced the format as a way to launch partisan attacks outside of the mainstream media.

PBS produced what many call the first "reality program" in 1973, An American Family, which depicted seven months in the lives of the Loud family. MTV created a hit with The Real World, and a decade later, the smashing success of Survivor opened the floodgates of reality programming on network television. The long and the short of it demonstrates that reality programming is no passing fad, instead generating unending concepts for the weird and unusual, as well as the thoughtful and insightful.

Visit Vault at **www.vault.com** for insider company profiles, expert advice, career message boards, expert resume reviews, the Vault Job Board and more.

VAULT CAREER LIBRARY   95

INNOVATIVE SOLUTIONS

David Collins
Founder, SCOUT

Important Stories, Well Told

Challenge

In the early 90s, some of my colleagues and I had an epiphany. We had spent many years working our way through the studio system and had attained highly respected production jobs, but we came to the realization that the stories we had been telling were no longer motivating enough. They just weren't enough to feel like, "Wow I'm willing to live on the road to keep working for the studios." Braving subzero temperatures in the middle of February during the filming of a major studio film in Two Harbors, Minnesota, we decided to grab hands and jump off the cliff. We left our well-paying, highly respected studio production jobs to go start Scout Productions.

Strategy & Solutions

At the time the core philosophy of the company was to tell important stories. 'Well told' was our mantra and still is after all these years. We started out in Boston for a couple of reasons. One, we had been living in LA and New York and fighting that system for quite a while, so we thought, let's be the big fish in a little pond. Two, we realized it was an amazing opportunity for material with all of the surrounding universities in Boston. The city was home to a plethora of smart, very creative young people. We started out in New England at the end of 1993 in Boston in the second floor guest bedroom of my house. That truly was the beginning. We incorporated in 1993 under Scout Productions, Inc. as a feature-film development company.

Little did we know of the big black holes that loomed in the world of development. It was naiveté and good old-fashioned entrepreneurial spirit that guided us. It was about grabbing hold of your own life and taking control.

It took me almost two years to realize that while everything I was doing on the business side was smart and right, if I didn't have the content first, the business side didn't matter. If you don't have the idea, the passion behind the company first, it doesn't matter at all what the business model is, because it is not going to work. You have to have the content first and then the business piece will fall into place.

In this day and age, do you need the business to be a close second? Yes. In the big picture, has business been elevated because of the approach towards brands now and how they are crafted within the production in advance? Yes. As long as you have that idea and then you start with that idea from the ground level up, the business opportunities will reveal themselves, so you understand how to take it to the next level.

About three or four years ago, as the company had evolved from just film, I had a vision. I really wanted to figure out how we were going to bring various media together as more and more people started talking about broadband and wireless. I wanted to understand how people are going to interact with their media and television in particular. The whole traditional broadcast and film models started to shake up a bit.

At the time we saw the opportunity for *Queer Eye for the Straight Guy* we had no true interest in just making a make-over show. We crafted it to be a "make better" show. The idea was based on the fact that you weren't going to change people into something they are not, but rather helping them to better their lives. In addition, we saw a real opportunity to push this idea a little further, so it wouldn't just be a TV show, but would also have all the ancillary opportunities of publishing, music, etc. The show was crafted from the beginning that way, so not only was there the core creative idea of the show, but we also identified all the business opportunities and models.

On the television side of Scout, that model has worked very well for lots of our shows.

It pushed our company to be "Scout, the evolution of media." There is a productions division, which handles film, television and music. There is a solutions division, which handles brand management, brand integration, marketing services and what we call a creative think tank, an innovation lab that encompasses licensing and merchandising.

Our overall company structure has changed. This isn't your daddy's production company anymore. While productions are productions and we know the formula of production inside and out, we've now been able to find the umbilical cord between solutions and productions, which takes the brand management and applies those principals to film, television and music.

Results

Bottom line, we are now going into our fifteenth year here because the mantra of important stories well told has not changed. Basically we were a film company that saw an opportunity in reality television, took it and had success. Queer Eye is a brand, it is an entire kind of philosophy that extended itself beyond one television show. It has now reached 102 countries and the brand has extended into merchandising, licensing, publishing and music.

There is Scout, "the evolution of media," in which we realized important stories well told cross all media, including film, TV and now in the wonderful world of new media opportunities. We are able to take everything we've learned over the years and apply it in a much larger and broader way using all of the pipelines that are now available to us.

Visit Vault at **www.vault.com** for insider company profiles, expert advice, career message boards, expert resume reviews, the Vault Job Board and more.

VAULT CAREER LIBRARY   97

The Inside Scoop

Must see

Following is a list of renowned documentary filmmakers. Viewing their work can help you better understand the variety of structures, elements and methods used to produce documentary films.

- Emile de Antonio
- Alan Berliner
- Les Blank
- Ken Burns
- Ric Burns
- Frank Capra
- Alberto Cavalcanti
- Debra Chasnoff
- Edward Curtis
- Peter Davis
- Arthur Dong
- Robert Drew
- John Else
- Robert Flaherty
- Susan Froemke
- Liz Garbus
- William Greaves
- John Grierson
- Patricio Guzman
- Henry Hampton
- Deborah Hoffmann
- Joris Ivens
- Steven James
- Humphrey Jennings
- Isaac Julien

- Jim Klein
- Barbara Kopple
- Claude Lanzmann
- Pare Lorentz
- Albert and David Maysles
- Errol Morris
- Michael Moore
- Dennis O'Rourke
- Lourdes Portillo
- Jean Rouch
- Frederick Wiseman
- Basil Wright
- Terry Zwigoff

Must read

Documentary Explorations; 15 Interviews with Film-Makers
by G. Roy Levin

Documentary Filmmakers Speak
by Liz Stubbs

Documentary: A History of the Non-Fiction Film
by Erik Barnouw

Film and Propaganda in America: A Documentary History
by David Culbert

Nonfiction Film: A Critical History
by Richard Meran Barsam

Public Television: Politics and the Battle Over Documentary Film
by B.J. Bullert

The Documentary Idea: A Critical History of English-Language Documentary Film and Video
by Jack C. Ellis

Western Civilization: A Critical Guide to Documentary Films
by Neil M. Heyman

Speak the language

Compressed Time: The compression of time between sequences or scenes, and within scenes. This is the most frequent manipulation of time in films; it is achieved with cuts or dissolves.

Cutaway: A bridging, intercut shot between two shots of the same subject. It represents a secondary activity occurring at the same time as the main action.

Dissolve: Also referred to as a mix; involves fading out one picture while fading up another on top of it.

Establishing Shot: Opening shot or sequence, frequently an exterior 'general view' as an extreme long shot. Used to set the scene.

Fade: The picture gradually appears from (fades in) or disappears to (fades out) a blank screen.

Following Pan: The camera swivels (in the same base position) to follow a moving subject. A space is left in front of the subject: the pan 'leads' rather than 'trails.'

Visit Vault at **www.vault.com** for insider company profiles, expert advice, career message boards, expert resume reviews, the Vault Job Board and more.

VAULT CAREER LIBRARY   99

Inset: An inset is a special visual effect in which a reduced shot is superimposed on the main shot. Often used to reveal a close-up detail of the main shot.

Jump Cut: Abrupt switch from one scene to another. May be used deliberately to make a dramatic point.

Long Shot: Shot which shows all or most of a fairly large subject and usually much of the surroundings.

Medium Shot: The subject and its setting occupy roughly equal areas in the frame.

Motivated Cut: Cut made just at the point where what has occurred makes the viewer immediately want to see something which is not currently visible. A typical feature is the shot/reverse shot technique (cuts coinciding with changes of speaker).

Point-of-View Shot (POV): A sequence that is shot as if the camera were looking through the eyes of a specific character

Reaction Shot: Any shot, usually a cutaway, in which a participant reacts to action which has just occurred.

Selective Focus: Rendering only part of the action field in sharp focus through the use of a shallow depth of field.

Soft Focus: An effect in which the sharpness of an image, or part of it, is reduced by the use of an optical device.

Surveying Pan: The camera slowly searches the scene, building to a climax or anticlimax.

Tilt: A vertical movement of the camera, up or down, while the camera mounting stays fixed.

Viewpoint: The apparent distance and angle from which the camera views and records the subject.

Wide-Angle Shot: A shot of a broad field of action taken with a wide-angle lens.

Wipe: An optical effect marking a transition between two shots. It appears to supplant an image by wiping it off the screen.

Join the club

Association of Independent Video and Filmmakers
Phone: 212-807-1400
www.aivf.org

DVD Association
www.dvda.org

IFP
Phone: 310-432-1200
www.ifp.org

International Documentary Association
Phone: 213-534-3600
www.documentary.org

Media Communications Association-International
Phone: 608-827-5034
www.mca-i.org

National Cable and Telecommunications Association
Phone: 202-775-3550
www.ncta.com

Women in Film and Video
Phone: 202-429-WIFV
www.wifv.org

Festivals

Cannes International Film Festival
www.festival-cannes.fr

Chicago International Film Festival
www.chicagofilmfestival.org

Dallas Video Festival
www.videofest.org

Denver International Film Festival
www.denverfilm.org

Docfest – New York International Documentary Festival
www.docfest.org

Visit Vault at **www.vault.com** for insider company profiles, expert advice,
career message boards, expert resume reviews, the Vault Job Board and more.

VAULT CAREER LIBRARY   **101**

Hollywood Film Festival
www.hollywoodawards.com

ResFest Digital Film Festival
www.resfest.com

Sundance Film Festival
www.sundance.org

Tribeca Film Festival
www.tribecafilmfestival.org

Job leads

Craigslist: www.craigslist.com
Click on desired city and then click on TV/Film/Video under "Jobs"

DocumentaryFilms.net: www.documentaryfilms.net/filmmakers.htm
Search a variety of resources to help launch your career in documentary filmmaking.

IFP Job Listings: www.ifp.org/jobs/

International Documentary Association:
www.documentary.org/resources/jobs_and_opps.php

LA411: www.la411.com/
Click on "Production Companies" to search for potential job leads.

Mandy: www.mandy.com

Media-Match: www.media-match.com/viewjobs.php

NY411: www.newyork411.com/
Click on "Production Companies" to search for potential job leads.

New England Film: www.newenglandfilm.com/jobs.htm

ProductionHub: www.productionhub.com/jobs/

Keep Your Career Moving Forward

Special training

There are several different paths for developing skills necessary for a successful career in documentary filmmaking. Some prefer the academic route, attending film or journalism school, while others opt for a training program at an academy or a similar nonacademic environment. Still others go with their gut and teach themselves how to use a digital camera and editing software. For those not ready to make the investment in equipment, there are now local schools and camera shops that rent out cameras or provide computers for editing.

Selected training programs:

Bay Area Video Coalition: www.bavc.org

Cyber Film School: www.cyberfilmschool.com

DVDojo: www.dvdojo.com

Graduate Program in Documentary Film and Video in Stanford University's Department of Communication: communication.stanford.edu/documentary/

NY Film Academy: www.nyfa.com

The Documentary Institute at the University of Florida: www.jou.ufl.edu/documentary

The Film/Video Department at Columbia College Chicago: www.filmatcolumbia.com

Tisch School of the Arts: www.tisch.nyu.edu

UCLA School of Theater, Film and Television: www.tft.ucla.edu/index.cfm

Landing your first job

There isn't a clearly defined path for building a career in documentaries. It is the most entrepreneurial of all media. Success in this field depends on both your talent and your persistence. Just pick up a digital video camera and start shooting! Following are some alternative entry points into documentaries:

Commercials: Diehard documentary filmmakers may regard you as a sell out, but just as many got their start producing commercials. The short length of commercials gives you the opportunity to practice the basics of filmmaking over and over, including lighting, sound and shooting.

Corporate Videos: Major companies now regularly hire production companies to produce a wide array of videos outside of their traditional marketing and advertising efforts. They have videos produced to enhance corporate communications initiatives, including internal training videos, DVDs demonstrating their products or services as part of sales kits, coverage of meetings or conferences for employees who were unable to attend, and online video for their various web sites. It's not always the most exciting content, but it pays well and can help supplement your income while you wait for your big break.

Getting your career unstuck

You may think you have the best idea in the world, but you may discover as you shop it around that there is no audience for it. As you develop your idea, you should also be developing your pitch to sell it. If you approach a cable channel or a public station, try to find out what kind of content they are currently seeking for their upcoming schedule. If you want to produce a documentary on emergency rooms, and the channel to which you are pitching has just aired a documentary on hospitals, chances are they will be less than enthusiastic about your idea.

You also want to make sure there is a measurable audience for your documentary. If the topic is too obscure, networks will most likely pass on it. If you happen to be told that your idea will draw too small an audience for television, consider direct distribution via the Internet or DVD. These new forms of distribution offer the opportunity to target niche audiences.

Consider pitching a series, several different episodes tied together with a common theme like food or nature. With more time to fill than ever before, cable channels in particular are interested in quantity, but unfortunately not always quality, which may or may not work in your favor.

Public Relations

The public relations industry has grown vastly in scope over the last decade. It has moved beyond simply drafting press releases for the launch of a new product or doing damage control for a corporate entity, tasks most commonly associated with the profession. The practice of public relations has become more and more sophisticated as the media world has grown in complexity.

Public relations is not only about generating buzz or maintaining an image, but also about complex strategic communications. Once regarded as "practitioners" crafting communications and messages for press releases, public relations professionals have now widened their scope. With a growing focus on the business and strategic impact of communications, the industry's role grows more important with every passing day.

What makes public relations unique?

The most striking difference of public relations compared with other sectors of information media is its lack of a designated distribution channel for its content. In fact, it is dependent on all of the available media outlets to help spread the information it has gathered on behalf of its clients. Public relations practitioners work with journalists at television stations, magazines, newspapers, web sites and radio stations to get their message out. However, while in public relations, information is gathered to help develop and implement a communications strategy on behalf of a paying client, journalists gather information to be shared with the communities they serve.

What attracts people to work in public relations?

Public relations practitioners are advocates for business, nonprofits, governments and other organizations to help those entities better communicate with the public. Their primary role is to understand the world around them, anticipating trends that will affect their clients or the organization they represent.

Those attracted to the industry are generally strategic thinkers who enjoy the challenge of crafting a message to meet the communications goals of an organization. Of course, there's no denying that schmoozing is a must in this

Visit Vault at **www.vault.com** for insider company profiles, expert advice, career message boards, expert resume reviews, the Vault Job Board and more.

VAULT CAREER LIBRARY   **105**

industry; convincing journalists to write about your client is a talent unto itself.

On the agency side, or internally at a company, public relations professionals help organizations better understand how the marketplace perceives them, and how to best relate to its various shareholders, including its employees, customers, stockholders and anyone else with a vested interest in the company. Developing and maintaining a wide variety of relationships is another crucial responsibility of a public relations professional.

Is a Career in Public Relations for You?

Lifestyle

Working in public relations can be a lot of fun, especially if you enter in on the entertainment or consumer products side, but it's also a lot of hard work. The hours are long and your work doesn't always fit neatly between 9 a.m. and 5 p.m. Generally, there is a lot of travel involved. The pay is low to start, but if you stick it out, it can become quite lucrative. Since it's a business based on relationships, it generally appeals to outgoing people. It also attracts "type A" personalities who have an eye for details.

Desired skills & traits

Creativity: Unlike advertising, you aren't paying to place your message in a magazine, newspaper or broadcast, so your creativity will come into play as you think of different angles to get journalists to write about your story.

Being Proactive: Rule number one in public relations – never sit back and wait. Always think ahead and anticipate different scenarios that may affect the message you are crafting.

Good Judgment: A good portion of the information you will deal with in public relations is highly sensitive. Always remember who you are talking to and what level of information you are able to provide them.

Analytical Skills: With volumes of data to get through each day, you must be able to cite trends and summarize information you have gathered into key points.

People Skills: This is an industry in which you definitely don't want to burn any bridges. The value of your career is measured in relationships.

Career Track

Basic duties

Staying Informed: If you have an insatiable appetite for news, you'll love this career. Reading a variety of newspapers every day is a must. Consume information from any and all sources as it relates to your clients or the organization you represent, including the mainstream press, trade magazines, web sites, chat rooms, discussion boards, online newsletters and industry conferences.

Organization: As they say, the devil is in the details! With the massive amount of information you will need to organize, every bit of information is vital, and you'll always need to have it at your fingertips. You will also be responsible for organizing meetings, press conferences, panel discussions and other major events.

Communications: The majority of your time will be spent communicating verbally or in writing. There is no better place to learn the art of a well written memo than in public relations. At the very least, a stint in public relations will greatly enhance your communication skills.

Listening: Probably the most overlooked part of great communication skills.

Anticipation: The bulk of public relations used to be focused on "spinning." or reacting to a situation and then developing a response. More and more, public relations has shifted towards thinking ahead, analyzing trends, reducing surprises and developing more effective communication strategies.

Entry level

Salary Range: $22,000 to $30,000

Track: Assistant, Assistant Account Executive

Yes, you will be overwhelmed by a variety of tedious tasks, but it is a great opportunity to learn your way around an office, especially if you've never worked in one before. You will also start learning the basics of public relations by managing endless details like traveling arrangements and your boss' schedule, and organizing meetings. Most people spend no more than a year as an assistant. If you don't know PowerPoint yet, learn. Also, the photocopier and the IT staff will become your best friends.

Visit Vault at **www.vault.com** for insider company profiles, expert advice, career message boards, expert resume reviews, the Vault Job Board and more.

VAULT CAREER LIBRARY   **107**

Mid-career

Salary Range: $30,000 to $60,000

Track: Account Executive, Senior Account Executive, Account Supervisor, Senior Account Supervisor

By this point in your career you finally have your own business cards, and, if you're lucky, a shared assistant. At this level you are given more responsibility and more autonomy. Responsibilities include day-to-day interaction with clients, writing press releases and other communications materials, and arranging press events.

Some public relations professionals begin moving from the agency side of the business into positions on the client side at this level. Many work in the communications departments of corporations. Some also enter the government, working as press secretaries.

Management or specialization

Salary Range: $75,000 and up

Track: Vice President, Senior Vice President, General Manager, President

You've made it! You have mastered your trade. Primary responsibilities include developing new business, maintaining relationships with high-level clients, developing highly sensitive communication strategies, and in some cases, management of the firm as a whole.

At this level, many public relations professionals develop their specialty even further, becoming a communications expert in a particular field like health, finance or consumer products. Some move onto the client side to run corporate communications departments or to become an investor relations executive. Those with a more entrepreneurial spirit go off on their own, finding their own clients and starting their own firms.

INSIGHTS FROM INDUSTRY LEADERS

Nancy Turett

President and Global Director, Edelman Health

Nancy Turett oversees five health specialty practices, Rx Health, Consumer Health, Life Sciences, Health Policy & Public Affairs and BioScience Communications, which is Edelman's medical and education publishing firm. Edelman is the world's leading independent public relations agency, offering a full range of communications services, with PR at the center with annual billings over $135 million. Some of Edelman's healthcare clients include Pfizer, Johnson & Johnson, Schering-Plough and Abbott.

Q: Do you think that "public relations" is still an adequate term to describe what your industry does now?
A: No, I don't. For people who are sophisticated public relations practitioners, it's a fine term, because we define it as how we actually live it and do it, but as a term for people who are not as familiar with public relations, it's actually limiting. They either think A) PR means press release, not public relations, or B) they think it means a relationship with the public rather than many publics.

Edelman used to be Edelman Public Relations Worldwide, and now we're just Edelman, and I actually led the process of changing our name. Along with a lot of other people here, and many of our clients who we surveyed, I thought "public relations" was too narrow a term for what we do. Having said that, PR is still a good shorthand for what we do because it is what we do.

Q: As the Internet has made information more available, how do you address both the challenge of managing proprietary information and keeping your client's message focused?
A: Those are two important questions. The first answer is that you can't really manage it. What you need to do is recognize that you can't own or control the situation, but you can ensure that you're communicating clearly, specifically and consistently enough to have the promulgation of your message not get too distorted.

The idea that you can actually control the message is a fallacy. The days of a company having one spokesperson are also over. Every employee is potentially a spokesperson for their company, official or de facto. The democratization of communications started on the Internet, but it's now happening offline as well as online.

Q: Media professionals consume an incredible amount of information every day. How do you stay informed?
A: My number one source of information is my BlackBerry. Other people funnel information over to me. When I think about what keeps me connected to the world, my BlackBerry comes first and my phone comes second. Actually, even ahead of the BlackBerry are people.

I definitely read *The New York Times* and *The Wall Street Journal* every day, and I read the headlines of *The Financial Times*. I scan all kinds of electronic services that give me headlines in my email.

The way to be on top of things is to be in the world. For example, when I walk out of my office, there are lots of people staring up at the JumboTron in Times Square, getting their news in real time. When I read the New York Times, it's to get depth, not to find out what happened in the world; I already know that because I saw it on my BlackBerry when I woke up in the morning.

Visit Vault at **www.vault.com** for insider company profiles, expert advice, career message boards, expert resume reviews, the Vault Job Board and more.

VAULT CAREER LIBRARY   **109**

Understanding the Industry

Current trends

High Growth: Employment for the public relations profession is expected to increase faster than the average growth rate for all other occupations through 2012.

More Strategic: The role of public relations has grown beyond simply pitching press releases to journalists and spinning messages to portray clients in a more favorable light. Increasingly, communication practices within public relations have become more strategic as the brand identity of corporations gains importance.

Proliferation of Information: The Internet has complicated the ability of public relations professionals to craft and distribute their message. The transparency of the Internet has made more information available to more people than ever before, but the fragmentation of the media has also made it more challenging for public relations professionals to control their message and to make the message stand out.

At the same time, the Internet offers the public relations industry direct access to distribution, so it no longer has to rely exclusively on traditional media to help get the word out.

Industry Snapshot

Overall Value: $4 billion

Number Employed: 160,000

Number Self-Employed: 11,000

Growth: Increase in revenues of 13% in first quarter of 2004 from same period a year earlier.

Geographic Centers: New York, Los Angeles, Chicago, San Francisco and Washington, D.C.

Breaking Down Public Relations

Agencies: The most common route into the public relations field is to join a public relations firm. Firms pitch their communication services to clients ranging from corporations to nonprofit organizations to government agencies. These services include organizing press events, writing press releases, launching new products, publishing, providing "damage control" for corporate missteps or miscommunication, as well as a variety of other strategic support.

Corporate Communications: Also referred to as the "client side" in the public relations world. There are two primary corporate communications roles, media relations and investor relations. Media relations focuses on relationships with media outlets like newspapers and television stations. Investor relations focuses on those shareholders with a financial stake or interest in the company, like stockholders, financial analysts and potential investors. Some senior executives in this field develop and maintain the overall corporate communications strategy.

Publicists: A public relations function in which the communications needs of a single individual, such as an author or other celebrity, is served. Referred to as press secretaries in politics. Publicists manage all relations with the media, promote their client's activities (or downplay them in some cases) and manage their public schedule.

Key Players

Brodeur Worldwide
855 Boylston Street
Boston, MA 02116
Phone: 617-587-2800
Web: www.brodeur.com

Burson Marsteller
230 Park Avenue South
New York, NY 10003
Phone: 212-614-4000
Web: www.bm.com/pages/home

Visit Vault at **www.vault.com** for insider company profiles, expert advice, career message boards, expert resume reviews, the Vault Job Board and more.

VAULT CAREER LIBRARY   111

Cohn & Wolfe
292 Madison Avenue
New York, NY 10017
Phone: 212-798-9700
Web: www.cohnwolfe.com

Edelman Worldwide
1500 Broadway
New York, NY 10036
Phone: 212-768-0550
Web: www.edelman.com

Euro RSCG Corporate Communications
350 Hudson Street
New York, NY 10014
Phone: 212-886-2000
Web: www.eurorscg.com

Fleishman-Hillard Inc.
200 N. Broadway
St. Louis, MO 63102
Phone: 314-982-7725
Web: www.fleishman.com

GCI GROUP/APCO Worldwide
825 Third Avenue
New York, NY 10022
Phone: 212-537-8000
Web: www.gcigroup.com

Golin/Harris International
111 East Wacker Drive, 10th Floor
Chicago, IL 60601
Phone: 312-729-4000
Web: www.golinharris.com

Hill and Knowlton, Inc.
466 Lexington Ave., 3rd Floor
New York, NY 10017
Phone: 212-885-0300
Web: www.hillandknowlton.com

Ketchum, Inc.
1285 Avenue of the Americas
New York, NY 10019
Phone: 646-935-3900
Web: www.ketchum.com

Manning, Selvage & Lee
1675 Broadway
New York, NY 10019
Phone: 212-468-4200
Web: www.mslpr.com

Ogilvy Public Relations Worldwide
909 Third Avenue
New York, NY 10022
Phone: 212-880-5200
Web: www.ogilvypr.com

Porter Novelli
450 Lexington Avenue
New York, NY 10017
Phone: 212-601-8000
Web: www.porternovelli.com

Ruder Finn Group
301 East 57th St.
New York, NY 10022
Phone: 212-593-6423
Web: www.ruderfinn.com

Waggener Edstrom, Inc.
Three Centerpointe Drive
Suite 300
Lake Oswego, OR 97035
Phone: 503-443-7000
Web: www.wagged.com

Weber Shandwick Worldwide
640 5th Ave.
New York, NY 10019
Phone: 212-445-8000
Web: www.webershandwick.com

Visit Vault at www.vault.com for insider company profiles, expert advice,
career message boards, expert resume reviews, the Vault Job Board and more.

VAULT CAREER LIBRARY   113

INNOVATIVE SOLUTIONS

Michael J. Mitchell

Director, Corporate Communications, The Medicines Company

Communicating the Complex to a Diverse Audience: Clinical Trial Results Press Releases

---

The Challenge

A major ongoing business challenge for corporate communications professionals is to communicate complex concepts to a diverse audience of key stakeholders. This challenge is particularly pronounced for the host of publicly traded technology and emerging healthcare companies. The Medicines Company is one such publicly traded healthcare company.

We are a pharmaceutical company that concentrates in the acute care hospital markets. Our marketed product, Angiomax® (bivalirudin) is an intravenously-administered pharmaceutical used to prevent blood clotting during angioplasty procedures. We are developing Angiomax in several additional uses and have a pipeline of potential additional hospital products.

To develop pharmaceutical products, our company engages in a rigorous scientific process to evaluate product attributes. The most visible piece of the product development process is the conduct and results of clinical trials. Positioning and promoting clinical trial results is the most important function of healthcare corporate communications.

Well-constructed clinical trials usually yield simple answers to key product questions posed by physician customers. Getting to the simple answers, however, requires rigorous scientific data analyses that yield more complex answers than "yes it works" or "no it doesn't." Communications professionals in the healthcare industry are participating in a deep scientific discourse that ultimately positions products and companies.

Enormous resources are invested into openly sharing and explaining clinical and statistical data analysis of clinical trials with physicians, who are trained in, and understand, many of the subtle aspects of clinical trial conduct. The corporate communications resource investment seeks to explain clinical trial results to stakeholders, some of whom are lay people with limited or no medical training.

Thus, the challenge is to communicate complex concepts with simplicity. The key product and company stakeholders include investors, employees, customers (physicians and patients), and the media, who serve as a conduit to the public.

Strategy & Solutions

The primary vehicle for communicating clinical trial results to key stakeholders is the press release. The term "press release" is a misnomer – the press release is actually a tool for communicating real time information to all of the key stakeholders above. Even though there are other ways to address each of these stakeholders, the press release remains the first way – and the highest profile way – to communicate news to stakeholders.

At The Medicines Company, we tackle the challenge of creating press releases that communicate often complex clinical trial results to an audience with diverse interests by prioritizing the audiences we need to reach, then tailoring content to reach that primary audience.

It may come as a surprise to members of the press that press releases are not always written for them as the top priority, but it is a fact of life for corporate communications. We balance what may or may not be interesting to reporters with what may or may not be important to other stakeholders.

Prioritizing the audiences aids in the decision-making process of content management. Clinical trial results are a deep collection of data, with an equally deep qualitative description of what the data mean. Unfortunately, we cannot communicate the full scientific discourse in the form of a press release because of the needs for language selection appropriate for lay people, and length appropriate for a news story.

Results

Recently, we have developed a process that identifies the key data findings – the facts – and the qualitative description – the messages. Separating facts from messages has proven to be the most effective tool to elucidate what might be most important to stakeholders and/or interesting to media reporters.

We have found that the separation process helps us to develop our press releases with input from various internal and external sources. We also find that we create clearer releases for press and more informative releases for other stakeholders.

Visit Vault at **www.vault.com** for insider company profiles, expert advice, career message boards, expert resume reviews, the Vault Job Board and more.

V∧ULT CAREER LIBRARY   115

The Inside Scoop

Must read

MediaWeek: A weekly magazine covering all aspects of the media industry.
www.mediaweek.com

PR Week: News and features about the public relations industry.
www.prweek.com

PR News: A weekly newsletter with strategic ideas for public relations
professionals.
www.prandmarketing.com/subscribe.htm

A variety of individuals distribute their own online newsletters with news and
information about the public relations industry. Below are some of the most
prominent ones:

Entertainment PR Newsletter:
Email: darren@westcoastpr.com
Website: www.westcoastpr.com

Inside PR:
Email: pholmes@prcentral.com
Website: www.prcentral.com

Interactive Public Relations
Email: sarahm@ragan.com
Website: www.ragan.com

Investor Relations Newsletter
Website: www.kennedyinfo.com

Jack O'Dwyer's PR Newsletter
Email: jackodwyer@aol.com
Website: www.odwyerpr.com

Ragan Report
Email: davidm@ragan.com
Website: www.ragan.com

Speak the language

Backgrounder: An in-depth document that explains a product, service or company in the context of its need, place in the industry and place in history; often supports and explains an accompanying press release.

Bio: Biography (usually a brief synopsis of a person's credentials).

Boilerplate: Standard wording about a company that usually appears near the bottom of all company-issued press releases.

Buzz: Media and public attention given to a company, its products or services.

Call Tree: A list of names and contact information that should be notified immediately in a crisis.

Client List: A list of a company's key clients; sometimes includes contact information.

Collateral: Secondary documents that accompany or support PR deliverables.

Communications Audit: A systematic survey of members of a target audience (often members of the media or potential customers) to determine awareness of or reaction to a product, service or company.

Direct Mail: Communication sent by post or e-mail to a target audience.

Frequently Asked Questions (FAQ): A list of questions and answers for the media pertaining to a press release; often included in a press kit.

Fact Sheet: A short (generally one-page) document that provides a "snapshot" look at a company, product or service.

FUD: Short for "Fear, Uncertainty and Doubt." Using positioning of one's own products or services to cast fear, uncertainty and doubt on the competitor's.

Implied Endorsement: The character the public often assigns to non-paid neutral or positive media coverage of a company, its products or services.

Key Influencers: Individuals, groups or publications whose opinion or coverage of a product, service or company can significantly affect public perception within a specific market.

Noise: Confusion caused by too many messages trying to be delivered at one time.

Visit Vault at www.vault.com for insider company profiles, expert advice, career message boards, expert resume reviews, the Vault Job Board and more.

VAULT CAREER LIBRARY   117

Pitch: A prepared sales presentation, usually one-on-one (in public relations, it's generally an attempt to get positive coverage or analyst review).

Positioning: Placement of a company, its products or services in a market category or in relation to its competition.

Press Kit: Several press deliverables combined in one package (usually a folder).

Q&A: A document that lists predictions of difficult questions that may be posed to a company spokesperson, and the best answers the spokesperson can give to meet the company's objectives.

White Paper: A technical document that explains how a product or service functions and its purpose.

Join the club

Council of Public Relations Firms
Phone: 877-773-4767
www.prfirms.org

Public Relations Society of America
Phone: 212-460-1490
www.prsa.org

Institute for Public Relations
Phone: 352-392-0280
www.instituteforpr.com

International Association of Business Communicators
Phone: 415-544-4700
www.iabc.com

The Foundation of Women Executives in Public Relations
Phone: 212-859-7375
www.wepr.org

Job leads

PSRA Job Center
www.prsa.org/jobcenter/main/

MediaBistro
www.mediabistro.com

PRWeek Jobs
www.prweekjobs.com

West Coast PR Jobs
www.westcoastprjobs.com

Work In PR
www.workinpr.com

Keep Your Career Moving Forward

Special training

While not required, there has been a growing interest in public relations degrees over the last decade. Many who enter the business have a liberal arts degree or a communications background. Journalism is also a common track into public relations, but in fact, the industry attracts people with a wide variety of backgrounds. Many enter the industry as their second career, bringing expertise from fields like finance, healthcare, technology, journalism or consumer products.

Landing your first job

Like other media sectors over the last few years, public relations has taken a hit as well, but it is projected to experience rapid growth over the next decade.

Writing test: Many public relations firms require a test that includes copy editing and writing a press release. If you've never written a press release before, visit any corporate web site and read their press releases to get an idea of how to structure them. If you have written a press release in a previous capacity or have been published, be sure to include these materials with your resume and cover letter.

Multi-media skills: Mastering PowerPoint and developing basic web development skills will give you a huge competitive advantage in landing your first job. All public relations presentations are conveyed through PowerPoint. Learn it and love it. It will be a tool you will use frequently throughout your career.

Relations with the public: No longer the exclusive domain of a handful of New York firms and corporate spinmeisters, public relations is literally everywhere. Most organizations that deal with the public regularly or have a

Visit Vault at **www.vault.com** for insider company profiles, expert advice, career message boards, expert resume reviews, the Vault Job Board and more.

VAULT CAREER LIBRARY   119

significant community of shareholders now have communications specialists to manage the inflow and outflow of their information. If there is a particular industry or social cause you are interested in, contact companies in that area to see if they need help with their communications efforts.

Getting your career unstuck

Many public relations practitioners spend the early part of their careers paying their dues at a firm. Life on the agency side exposes you to a wide variety of clients, communications programs and media outlets. As in other media sectors, it is not uncommon to hop around, working for different firms to boost your salary and to gain more experience.

After five to ten years, some public relations professionals begin entering the management ranks or decide to apply their skills elsewhere. As your career progresses, be sure to develop a specialty; it is important to avoid general labels like "media relations person" or "writer." You will be valued more highly as an expert than as a generalist. If you work within a large firm, try to work on a project outside of your department to see what field most interests you, or put your public relations skills to use volunteering at a nonprofit organization.

Online Media

Online media is the place where all other media now intersect with one another. Throughout the history of media, the introduction of new technologies has always heightened fears about making existing technologies obsolete, but this has yet to happen. However, subsequent technologies do force established technologies to evolve and change, from the advent of radio, the first mass electronic medium in a media world exclusively dominated by print, to the rise of television. Now the Internet is leaving no traditional medium untouched by its influence.

Traditional media, first rattled by the perceived threat of the Internet, grew after the dot-com bust of 2000, but four years have now passed and the Internet is anything but a passing fad. In fact, it will dictate the future structure of all other mediums.

What makes online media unique?

What is so fascinating about the Internet compared with traditional mediums? Quite simply, it is its ability to give consumers unprecedented control over their media consumption, as well as a greater sense of involvement in the overall creative process. Traditional mediums, on the other hand rely on the concept of mass audiences, and traditional distribution channels.

What attracts people to work in online media?

The first wave of the Internet captured the imagination of entrepreneurs who set out to truly change age-old economic paradigms. While there was no shortage of ideas or cash behind the first websites, there was a severe shortage of sound business sense.

The emerging second wave of the Internet is backed by sound business fundamentals and focused creativity. The dot-com bust weeded out many non-media types, leaving a strong core of highly passionate individuals ready to meet the challenge of creating viable media businesses. Online media also emphasizes that the clearly defined division of labor in traditional media is slowly melting away. Of course, there will always be defined disciplines like IT specialist or writer, but lines between disciplines are increasingly blurry.

Is a Career in Online Media for You?

Lifestyle

Life at web companies has become more formal since the freewheeling days of just a few years ago, but the Internet companies still have a far more casual feel than other media sectors. Web entities controlled by traditional media companies may take on a similar culture as their parent, but there is still a distinct difference.

There is still a degree of risk in pursuing a career online, but the faithful would say that the pure fun of working within the online medium makes it all worthwhile. Others would argue that every day, the Internet grows and matures as traditional media loses focus and declines.

Desired skills & traits

Entrepreneurial Spirit: There are still very few successful Internet companies, but there are countless more survivors waiting in the wings to become household names like AOL, Google or Yahoo. These Internet successes saw something where no one else did, and had a lot of faith in their gut.

Ability to Sell: Even if you aren't on the frontlines selling advertising or services, selling your ideas internally is a crucial skill. New ideas are still flying around every day on the Internet. You need to be able to make a well-reasoned argument for your idea to rise to the top of the heap. Most importantly, you need to be able to articulate how much revenue your idea will generate, and the lower the cost, the better.

Team Player: As corny as it sounds, being able to work with others is key. Organizational hierarchy is less defined, and in many cases, so are individual roles. It's important to communicate well with others in the absence of these traditional divisions. More often than not, you will be working as a member of a small staff, so you will need to get along with everyone.

Career Track

Basic duties

Content Creation: Writers, web producers and community managers are primarily responsible for the creation of content, including articles, interactive applications and community-generated material. Most content-based websites' business models now depend on a mix of advertising and subscription, so new content is always needed to keep them growing.

Marketing: Marketers work closely with both the sales force and the creators of content to think of new creative and cost-effective ways to market a website's content and services. Successful marketing campaigns are based on Return On Investment (ROI). The return in sales has to exceed every dollar spent on marketing.

Selling: This function is not left to the sales force alone. Since the collapse of the dot-coms in 2000, surviving websites have made sales the supreme priority for all positions, because the company's survival depends on it. No, this does not mean web producers or designers are making cold calls, but sales is in the forefront of their thinking. When choosing between two different pieces of content, web producers will always favor the one they think will attract more users to the site.

Community Research: The beauty of the Web lies in immediate feedback from the community. Comments, traffic to different parts of the site, surveys and discussion boards are all constantly monitored to tailor the content to the target community's tastes, enhancing the overall marketing and sales efforts.

Design: Creating web pages is probably not part of your job description if you are a writer or a sales rep, but learning basic HTML and Photoshop will help make you more self-reliant, vastly expanding your opportunities and making your content or sales efforts that much more effective.

Visit Vault at **www.vault.com** for insider company profiles, expert advice, career message boards, expert resume reviews, the Vault Job Board and more.

VAULT CAREER LIBRARY   123

Content track

Production Assistant: Entry-level position. Help with administrative tasks, as well as with the basic maintenance of the site.

Salary Range: $20,000 to $25,000

Producer: Oversees the editorial direction of a specific section of a website. Develops new content in the form of articles, newsletters, discussion boards and databases.

Salary Range: $35,000 to $55,000

Writer: Generally a freelance position; writers conceive and develop written articles for websites. They may also be hired to write marketing messages or copy to enhance navigation of the site.

Salary: Varies depending on the project.

Community Manager: Interacts with website's target community on a daily basis.   Monitors discussion boards, chat rooms and other community applications. Also oversees the collection and management of community-generated content like polls, quizzes and other submitted content.

Salary Range: $45,000 to $55,000

Executive Producer: Supervises the editorial and production aspects of a website.

Salary Range: $60,000 and up

Business track

Assistant: Whether you are pursuing a career path in sales or marketing, there are entry-level positions available as an assistant in either department.

Salary Range: $20,000 to $25,000

Marketing Manager: Directs all marketing efforts to generate traffic for a website and its unique services. Marketing tools include direct e-mails, internal promotional messages, marketing barters with other sites, paid advertisements and direct marketing on search engines like Google.

Salary Range: $35,000 to $55,000

Sales Manager: Oversees all advertising revenue or revenue from a site's paid services. Sets monthly quotas for account executives, provides training, offers feedback and will often have client accounts of their own to manage.

Salary Range: $35,000 to $55,000 (plus commission)

E-commerce Manager: Manages development and growth of pay services for the site such as subscriptions, memberships or physical goods.

Salary Range: $35,000 to $55,000

Production track

Production Assistant: Entry-level position. Help design staff with basic HTML and other design maintenance issues.

Median Salary: $20,000

Designer: Responsible for designing all web pages, including pictures, special graphics, overall color scheme and branding elements for the site. Uses HTML, Quark, Flash and other design programs.

Salary Range: $35,000 to $50,000

Information Technology Manager (IT): Maintains technical structure of a website, including server, e-mail systems and desktop programs.

Salary Range: $45,000 to $55,000

Programmer: Creates databases, discussion boards, chat rooms and other interactive applications using Java/JSP, C++, .NET, ASP, SQL experience with Microsoft SQL and/or Oracle.

Salary Range: $45,000 to $80,000

INSIGHTS FROM INDUSTRY LEADERS:

Martin Nisenholtz

CEO, New York Times Digital

After serving as president of The New York Times Electronic Media Company since 1995, Nisenholtz was named CEO of New York Times Digital in June 1999. He oversees the development of NYTimes.com and the distribution of *The New York Times* content via other digital platforms. Prior to joining the Times, he served as director for content strategy for Ameritech Corporation.

Nisenholtz has a long and storied career in interactive media. While at Ogilvy & Mather Worldwide, he founded the Interactive Marketing Group (IMG) in 1983. It was the first creative development unit at a major U.S. advertising agency devoted specifically to interactive communication. Today he serves as the chairman of the Online Publishers Association and on the board of directors for the Interactive Advertising Bureau.

Q: What are the key ingredients for a well-designed news website today?

A: I think the key ingredients are the same that they've been for a while with maybe one exception. I think that the first and most important consideration is that the website more or less anticipates the information needs of the user. By that I mean that users come to news websites for different reasons at different times of the day. Your site needs to be designed to anticipate all of those need states.

The change in the last 18 months has been brought on by higher speed connections. While I don't think a lot of people come to us specifically because they think they want to hear our journalists in an interview or look at a video or a slide show, we think it's in our best interests to start providing those things, so people will eventually get used to wanting those elements. Fifty years ago, they didn't see many photographs in the paper, and now they see dozens and dozens every day. There's a give and take between what users really need and what they want.

Q: Do you see weblogs becoming an integral part of an online newspaper?

A: Yes, I do think that they can become an important part of a news website. It's always been our role to point to or aggregate what we consider to be valuable content. That can be done in a variety of different ways. I can easily envision having a weblog critic on nytimes.com or in the paper even, reviewing blogs the same way we have book reviewers or film reviewers.

To me, weblogs are a legitimate publishing activity and they're becoming more legitimate as the days go by, as more professionals get in and make them exciting and useful. I can imagine aggregating weblogs in certain categories so we're covering areas of the news that webloggers are particularly good at covering. I don't want to suggest that we're doing that at the Times right now; it's just something I've thought about as a way we could work with weblogs.

Q: There's an argument that if all news is made on demand, users will only read about their specific view of the world. Have you found this to be the case with NYTimes.com users?

A: No. The paper is an extremely powerful serendipitous reading experience. The whole notion, at least today and for the foreseeable future, that this is a zero-sum game where people either just read the paper or just read the website is simply wrong. There's no data to actually support this notion. Most people just read the paper. Some of the people who read the paper also read the website. Those who read the website probably also read a paper, maybe their own community newspaper.

I don't know what newspapers our 14.5 million users are reading, but I suspect most of them are also reading papers for the very reason you suggested: you can't get that serendipitous reading experience on a PC or a cell phone. They're completely different experiences even though they share some of the same content. It's not useful to think of them as zero-sum.

Visit Vault at **www.vault.com** for insider company profiles, expert advice, career message boards, expert resume reviews, the Vault Job Board and more.

VAULT CAREER LIBRARY   127

Understanding the Industry

Current trends

Growth & Rebound: The second wave of the Internet is be rising out of the ashes of the crash just four years ago. Internet advertising is projected to top $9 billion for 2004, approaching the highs of the Internet boom. More and more advertisers are also putting their ad dollars online. In September 2004, Mitsubishi North America announced that it was pulling its entire ad budget of $120 million from network television and redistributing it among cable, magazines and the Internet. Google's IPO in 2004 was the most anticipated IPO since 2000, a sign that investors are taking a closer look at the Internet once again.

RSS: Real Simple Syndication is an emerging method of distributing content across the Internet. Consumers download "news aggregators," pulling content from across the web that is of interest to them, rather than surfing on their own or depending on e-mailed newsletters.

Community-Generated Content: The phenomenon of weblogs has empowered individuals to share details of their day-to-day lives, inside information and creative expressions. Bloggers have also filled in the gap increasingly left by professional journalists, staying on top of stories forgotten by the mainstream media or exposing their mistakes.

Moblogs: A close cousin to blogs, they enable people to share their digital photos and pictures taken with their camera phones. Over time, professional journalists may assume responsibility for managing community-generated content, offering perspective and analysis for the overwhelming supply of information available to consumers.

Online Video: Broadband is now in more than 30 million U.S. homes, half of all homes with access to the Internet. High-speed access has now made the distribution of large video files across the Internet more viable, dramatically decreasing download times and improving the quality of video. This is all a boon for advertisers, who have long hoped to combine the emotional power of video with the interactivity of the Internet.

Industry Snapshot

Total Industry Ad Revenues for 2004: $9 billion

Growth: Online ad spending grew by 40% in the first half of 2004 compared with first half of 2003

Geographic Centers: San Francisco, New York, Los Angeles, Chicago, Boston and Washington, D.C.

Breaking Down Online Media

Extensions of Traditional Media: Most newspapers, broadcasters and publishers made a reluctant entry onto the Internet. But high valuations of web properties in the late 1990s made corporate executives at traditional operations see green, so they eventually made a mad dash online. Once regarded as separate business, online operations have now been rolled back into the traditional corporate structure. Even today, most traditional operations regard their websites as afterthoughts, a placeholder for their overall brand in the online world.

There is still a lack of understanding and an unwillingness to divert precious resources to unproven businesses. The design of many websites still reflect this entrenched thinking; newspapers tend to present their information online as they would for their print edition, and television websites simply copied the newspaper's strategy for presenting content. Slowly but surely, some traditional outlets have come to regard investing in their websites as investing in their future.

Independent Web Entities: Many independent web companies went belly-up in 2000, turning out many beleaguered media professionals onto the street. Those lucky enough to keep their jobs were also disillusioned, but still had a paycheck. Over the last few years, the surviving companies have worked through their dot-com hangovers. Cost cutting, creative thinking and a whole lot of faith have enabled them to get their books in order. Though these companies are slowly beginning to hire again, the scale is nothing compared to that of just five years ago. Aside from the content giants of the Internet like Yahoo or AOL (which acquired Time Warner in 2000 and then ended up being reduced to a division of Time Warner in 2003), websites focused on content like Salon or MarketWatch have survived by focusing on highly specific content or maintaining a tightly knit community.

Visit Vault at **www.vault.com** for insider company profiles, expert advice, career message boards, expert resume reviews, the Vault Job Board and more.

VAULT CAREER LIBRARY 129

Non-Media Entities: When most people think of pursuing a career in media, they focus on landing a job in the media industry. Seems obvious enough, but the Internet has now given every company, in every industry, a 24/7 media presence outside of normal distribution channels. BMW has cleverly created a website called BMWfilms.com, presenting original film shorts on demand with its cars as the stars. Howard Dean's presidential campaign demonstrated the candidate's ability to cover his own campaign through a video site, Howard Dean TV, and the ability to unite his supporters using the interactive community tools of MeetUp.com. If you love media and are passionate about a particular company or organization, here's your chance to kill two birds with one stone.

On Your Own: In broadcast or print, working "on your own" typically means you are a freelancer waiting for the phone to ring. Some media professionals are lucky enough to turn their freelance gigs into a production company or an agency. The Internet now gives everyone access to the largest audience available, the world. Of course, building a viable media business is not quite that simple, but some individuals are making a go of it primarily through the use of weblogs. Some receive so much traffic they are able to sustain themselves by selling advertising.

Increasingly, the Internet will become an important barometer by which to gauge any given media professional's ability to draw a following or to build a core audience before being embraced by more traditional media outlets.

Key Players

ABC News Digital
77 West 66th St.
New York, NY 10023
Phone: 212-456-6200
Web: www.abcnews.com

AOL
22000 AOL Way
Dulles, VA 20166
Phone: 703-265-1000
Web: www.corp.aol.com

Advance.Net, Advance Publications
950 Fingerboard Rd.
Staten Island, NY 10305
Phone: 212-286-2860
Web: www.advance.net

Associated Press
450 West 33rd St.
New York, NY 10001
Phone: 212-621-1500
Web: www.ap.org

CBSMarketWatch
425 Battery St.
San Francisco, CA 94111
Phone: 415-733-0500
Web: cbs.marketwatch.com

CBSNews.com
524 West 57th St.
New York, NY 10019
Phone: 212-975-4321
Web: www.cbsnews.com

CNN
1 CNN Center
Atlanta, GA 30303
Phone: 404-827-1500
Web: www.cnn.com

Foxnews.com
1211 Avenue of the Americas
New York, NY 10036
Phone: 212-301-3000
Web: www.foxnews.com

Hearst Newspapers Digital
959 8th Ave.
New York, NY 10019
Phone: 212-649-2000
Web: www.hearst.com/newspapers

Visit Vault at www.vault.com for insider company profiles, expert advice,
career message boards, expert resume reviews, the Vault Job Board and more.

VAULT CAREER LIBRARY   131

Knight Ridder Digital
50 W. San Fernando St., Ste. 1500
San Jose, CA 95113
Phone: 408-938-7700
Web: www.knightridder.com/digital

MSNBC Interactive News
1 Microsoft Way
Redmond, WA 98052
Phone: 425-882-8080
Web: www.msnbc.com

New York Times Digital
500 7th Ave., 8th Floor
New York, NY 10018
Phone: 646-698-8000
Web: www.nytdigital.com

Reuters (U.S. Office)
3 Times Square
New York, NY 10036
Phone: 646-223-4000
Web: www.reuters.com

Salon Media Group
22 4th St., 11th Floor
San Francisco, CA 94103
Phone: 415-645-9200
Web: www.salon.com

The FeedRoom
205 Hudson St., 8th Floor
New York, NY 10013
Phone: 212-219-0343
Web: www.feedroom.com

USAToday.com
7950 Jones Branch Dr.
McLean, VA 22107-0910
Phone: 703-854-6000
Web: www.usatoday.com

WSJ Interactive

1 World Financial Center
200 Liberty St.
New York, NY 10281
Phone: 212-416-2000
Web: www.wjs.com

Washingtonpost.Newsweek Interactive

1515 N. Court House Rd.
Arlington, VA 22201-2909
Phone: 703-469-2500
Web: www.washingtonpost.com

Yahoo! Inc.

701 1st Ave.
Sunnyvale, CA 94089
Phone: 408-349-3300
Web: www.yahoo.com

Visit Vault at www.vault.com for insider company profiles, expert advice,
career message boards, expert resume reviews, the Vault Job Board and more.

VAULT CAREER LIBRARY   133

INNOVATIVE SOLUTIONS

Gail Ann Williams

Director of Communities, Salon.com

Guiding Online Communities Towards Profitability

The Challenge

Turning on a dime has its price. This spring, Salon undertook the unraveling of innovative solutions we'd wrought at Salon.com during the summer doldrums of 2001. At the time, while the online advertising market was faltering, Salon ran two vibrant forum sites. Members of The WELL, the venerable forum community Salon had acquired at our 1999 IPO, had always paid a membership fee. Earlier in 2001, we had initiated Salon Premium, a second subscription program for ad-fee reading of the professionally written portions of Salon.com. However, our forums at Salon Table Talk were still home to thousands of active non-paying participants.

Strategy & Solutions

We knew our Table Talkers had powerful group and brand loyalty. Most would never move to The WELL, with its different social structures and different interface peculiarities. In light of staff resources at that time, the one way to move quickly was to ask TTers to join The WELL in order to use those billing resources. We knew they'd have to retain Table Talk's contents and forum platform, so we cobbled the systems together and established a revenue-generating Table Talk group.

Since then, we've learned that Table Talkers expected Salon Premium subscriptions to be included, and vice versa. Few could get to know people on both The WELL and TT, so additional forum access was not seen as added value. This spring, we shifted TT over to become a benefit of Salon Premium to reduce customer confusion, ease support loads and make Salon more member-centric.

Customer confusion had been the impetus, so we wanted the project to flow from a picture of customer simplicity. We decided what we wanted to tell our customers about upcoming changes. After setting goals from the user experience perspective, we looked at the dissimilarities of the two custom databases in use for WELL and Salon Premium billing, and forged a data migration project. Our hurdles came from assumptions in one database that users may be identified by a unique e-mail address. The other database allows duplicate paid accounts and addresses.

Results

We survived the expected surge in demand for customer support after the fact. We've quadrupled participants in Table Talk in two months. Ongoing TTers liked the price reduction, and appreciated the new posters. Ongoing Salon Premium subscribers got a new benefit to try. We take pride in a more logical offer, simpler support, and progress towards intensifying the membership experience for our site as a whole.

Sometimes you have to respond nimbly to challenges in the short run. However, the emergency custom solution – the heroic IT hack – can become chaos deferred. When you must reinvent your site swiftly, imagine the eventual data export and clean up issues up front.

The Inside Scoop

Must read

CNET: Daily online resource for all the latest digital media and technology news.
www.cnet.com

CyberJournalist: Online resource providing journalists with information and tools on how to evolve their skills in a digital world.
www.CyberJournalist.net

Digital Media Wire: Daily newsletter covering top business stories about games, digital music, mobile entertainment and interactive television.
www.digitalmediawire.com

Internet.com: Online resource providing highly technical information about issues facing the Internet.
www.internet.com

Online Publishers Association Report: A bi-weekly online publication summarizing news and information affecting the online publishing industry.
www.online-publishers.org/newsletters.html

Streaming Media Xtra: Newsletter reporting on news and events as it pertains to streaming media.
www.streamingmedia.com

Wired: Monthly magazine covering a variety of technology issues and the digital lifestyle.
www.wired.com

Speak the language

Above the Fold: Refers to the part of the screen where a user does not have to scroll to see content.

Band Width: The size of the Internet pipe you have when you connect to the Web. If you are on a T1 line, you have access to a higher bandwidth than someone connecting with a 56kbps modem.

Blog: Previously referred to specific content management software (blogger), but now a description for a wide range of personal pages, journals, and diary-type setups.

Visit Vault at **www.vault.com** for insider company profiles, expert advice, career message boards, expert resume reviews, the Vault Job Board and more.

VAULT CAREER LIBRARY   135

Broadband: A network transmission method that uses a single divided medium so that multiple signals can travel across the same medium simultaneously.

Browser: The two most common browsers, Microsoft Internet Explorer and Netscape Navigator, interpret the HTML code and scripts, allowing you to view the graphics, color, and text in a web page.

CPM: Cost Per Thousand (think metric where M=T). CPM advertising models are based on advertisers purchasing page views in blocks of 1000.

Cache: Temporarily stores web pages you have visited in your computer. A copy of documents you retrieve is stored in cache.

Click Through: When a user selects a hyper text (web page) link. Many web statistics are kept on click-throughs (sometimes abbreviated as click-thru).

Conversion Rate: The relationship between visitors to sales or actions. If 1 person out of 100 purchases a site's product, it has a conversion rate of 1 to 100.

Cookie: A message from a web server computer, sent to and stored by your browser on your computer. The main function of cookies is to provide customized web pages according to a profile of your interests.

Domain Name: This is the web address or URL (Uniform Resource Locator) for a website.

GIF: A graphic file format for saving images on the web. GIF is best for art and drawings having flat, solid areas of color.

Hit: A request for a file on a webserver. Most often, these are graphic files and documents.

Impressions: The actual number of people who've seen a specific Web page. Impressions are sometimes called "page views."

Mirror Site: A shadow duplicate copy of a website at a separate URL. This allows websites to spread out the resource load on a server.

Page Views: Web Page Hits, or number of times a page is viewed.

Pop Under: A pop-up that loads under a page so that it is only viewable when the current page is closed.

Unique Visitors: A single individual website visitor. If you have high visitor counts, but relatively low page per user counts, that indicates that people are not finding your site attractive enough to read through it.

Real Simple Syndication (RSS): This is an XML-based Web syndication tool for Websites and blogs. RSS repackages new content with information such as a date, a title, a link, and a brief description. An RSS Reader then interprets this feed so that the user need only read the description and link to the news story or blog post.

Reciprocal Link: When two websites swap links to point at each other. Also known as a link exchange.

Join the club

Association for Interactive Marketing
Phone: 888-337-0008
Web: www.interactivehq.org

Interactive Advertising Bureau
Phone: 212-949-9033
Web: www.iab.net

Online Publishers Association
Phone: 646-698-8071
Web: www.online-publishers.org

Job leads

Craigslist
www.craigslist.com

MediaBistro
www.mediabistro.com

Vault
www.vault.com

Visit Vault at **www.vault.com** for insider company profiles, expert advice,
career message boards, expert resume reviews, the Vault Job Board and more.

VAULT CAREER LIBRARY   **137**

Keep Your Career Moving Forward

Special training

Whether you are pursuing a career in content, technology or business, there really are no required degrees. Obviously, special training is necessary to become a programmer, web designer or an IT administrator. Universities with art or technology programs, as well as special technical schools offer such training. Programs that are a must to know for designers are Flash, Quark, HTML and XML depending on the needs of the online organization.

Content-based websites like the NYTimes.com or ABCNews.com attract those who are interested in journalism or writing careers. As with other media, a journalism school degree isn't necessary, but it won't hurt.

On the business side, an entrepreneurial spirit is the most valuable trait you can offer an online company. A degree in marketing can help provide a foundation for your career, but most of the skills necessary for online marketing and sales can only be learned through real world experience that internships can offer.

Landing your first job

Your own creation: Nothing could impress a potential employer more than your very own website or weblog. Creating your own web entity demonstrates your passion for the medium and shows off your creative abilities. You also build your skills in the process.

Hands-on experience: Even if you are pursuing a career on the content or business side, knowing basic HTML and Photoshop are a huge plus. The online world is very team-driven and the various work roles within it are often less defined than in other media. It showcases your "can-do" spirit.

Bring ideas to the table: Creativity is now just as important on the business side as it is in content development. Certainly not to the extent of the creative accounting practices of Enron, but the online world is still in the formative stages of developing new business models. Thinking outside of the box is necessary to adapt traditional business sense to the brave new world of digital media.

No matter what position you are applying for, study the website thoroughly and be prepared to offer two or three ideas for the site in your interview.

Those applying for design jobs may be asked to provide examples of their work.

Getting your career unstuck

Much of the advice provided for other media also applies to the online world. Moving around, starting your own business or working in larger markets are all options to increase your pay and to gain more responsibility.

The outlook for the Internet is the brightest it has been since the dot-com bust of 2000. It offers big risks, but also big rewards. There are far more opportunities to push your creative abilities and career goals than in any other medium. For all intents and purposes, the Internet is still a fairly undefined medium, so there are far more opportunities to run with a new idea than in other media with more rigidly defined structures. Of course, even those on the content and technology sides need to prove how their ideas will make money for the site or help to improve its overall value. You can have all the brilliant ideas in the world, but if you can't show how they will make money, they will fall on deaf ears.

Visit Vault at **www.vault.com** for insider company profiles, expert advice, career message boards, expert resume reviews, the Vault Job Board and more.

VAULT CAREER LIBRARY   **139**

Children's Media

Children's media is a far cry from the days of *Howdy Doody* and *The Mickey Mouse Club*. Over the last decade kids' media has proliferated. In 1990, there was just one preschool television distributor; today there are six. Children's media has moved far beyond Saturday morning cartoons, PBS educational programming, a few annual movies and some books. Today it is all about delivering children's media brands anywhere, any way and anytime kids want them.

Children's media has grown to become a multibillion-dollar business. It is estimated that children between the ages of four and twelve spent or influenced purchases totaling $40 billon in 2002. Observing the "on-demand" media habits of kids today also offers a window into the future structure of media.

What makes children's media unique?

The business is based on marketing to a specific demographic – kids – rather than selling a medium like television or books. It's rare for a children's media concept to be limited to just one medium anymore. As soon as a concept is developed, writers, producers and other creative talent work with marketers to determine how to best translate the content and brand across multiple media channels. Generally, the creative forces determine what will and won't work. While one brand may translate better from television to the movies, it may make more sense for another brand to move from television to merchandising opportunities. It just has to make sense for the brand.

What attracts people to work in children's media?

The driving force that attracts media professionals to children's media is the love of children. Children's media also offers a rare opportunity to use the vehicle of entertainment to help mold young minds for the better. The imaginative nature of children gives writers, producers and illustrators the leeway to stretch their creative ideas in ways they might not be encouraged to if they were reaching out to adults.

Visit Vault at **www.vault.com** for insider company profiles, expert advice, career message boards, expert resume reviews, the Vault Job Board and more.

VAULT CAREER LIBRARY   141

Is a career in children's media for you?

If you don't like kids, consider another line of work. If the passion is not there, children will be the first to pick up on it, and you will not be a success in this business.

Pursuing a career in children's media offers you many different options, but also forces you to make more decisions about your career than might other media sectors. You must decide what track or general discipline most interests you. Are you more interested in content development, technology or the business side? Do you have a preference as to which medium you would prefer to work in, television, film, publishing, magazines or interactive media? Is there a specific age range – preschool, tweens or teenagers – that interests you more than another?

There are a wide range of basic duties determined by the discipline and path you choose. Your salary expectations will also be defined by those decisions. Most entry-level salaries are between $20,000 and $25,000.

Desired skills & traits

Love of Children: This point can't be emphasized enough.

Creativity: If you want to keep up with the latest tastes and trends of children, your imagination should be nearly as active as theirs, if not more so.

Ability to Observe and Listen: Children are still learning how to express themselves through words and often rely on other forms of expression to communicate themselves. It is important to pick up on these cues to capture the fuller picture of what children are trying to tell you, cues that may not be communicated by words alone.

Career Track

One of your first career choices in media is deciding which area you would predominantly like to work in. Children's media is evolving in such a way that you will most likely be brought into contact with various mediums, beyond the primary medium in which you started.

Publishing

If you love books, publishing is a great place to start. There are many different types of opportunities, from picture books to fiction and non-fiction. Career paths include becoming an illustrator, author, literary agent, editor or marketer. On the creative side, there are opportunities for freelancers to break into the industry, and aspiring authors should seek the counsel of an agent. There are entry-level positions available for those seeking a career as an editor or marketer, although the starting salary is very low.

Over the past two decades, study after study has shown that Americans of all ages are reading less and less. Many argue that the increased time spent on television, video games and the Internet is coming at the expense of reading newspapers and books. Many busy parents also don't take the time to encourage reading habits, either by reading to their children at bedtime or setting an example by nurturing their own reading habits.

There was some encouragement with the lightning-fast rise of Harry Potter, which broke publishing records and maybe even some myths about children's attitudes towards reading. Some of the Harry Potter books are thicker than a phone book, the longest almost 900 pages long! Boys were just as eager to read the series as girls, who are typically more interested in reading. Many parents and teachers believe the phenomenon has helped spark enthusiasm for reading, holding out hope that the magic of Harry Potter will sow the seeds of reading habits in a new generation.

Television

Although there are more children's programs than ever before, the world of children's television is still fairly small, making landing your first job highly competitive. Many of the opportunities lie in cable or at production companies that produce programming for broadcast and cable television. Over the last few years, publishers have also expanded their capacity for producing programming as they seek to move their characters to both the small and big screens.

On the production side, you might consider a path in producing, writing, design or illustrating. The business side has become more and more defined by marketing and brand management, as characters and shows are now regarded as brands. It is now the job of marketers to determine the most appropriate distribution channels or "touch points" to maximize the value of the brand, while not diluting it from a creative standpoint.

Visit Vault at **www.vault.com** for insider company profiles, expert advice,
career message boards, expert resume reviews, the Vault Job Board and more.

VAULT CAREER LIBRARY   **143**

Over the last decade, children's television programming has exploded beyond the once exclusive domain of PBS and Saturday morning cartoons on the networks, creating many new career opportunities. It now encompasses educational programming, cartoons, game shows, dramas and even reality shows.

Television for kids today has a much broader definition than it did just five years ago. Home videos and the proliferation of DVDs now enable kids to watch their favorite movies and shows whenever they want to. Soon their parents will be able to order those same programs via Video On Demand.

More and more kids will no longer know the boredom of long car rides during summer vacations, sitting in the back seat with nothing better to do than torture your sibling. Many cars are now equipped with video entertainment systems. Video media is everywhere for kids.

Founded in 1979, Nickelodeon has come to dominate children's television and has transformed children's media in the process. It has been the highest rated basic cable network since 1995, reaching over 80 million households, and has produced some of the hottest shows in children's television, like *Sponge Bob Square Pants*, *Bob the Builder* and *Blues Clues*. As part of the Viacom empire, Nickelodeon now powers the CBS Saturday Morning lineup with a slate of programming branded as "Nick Jr. on CBS." Many of the popular characters created by Nickelodeon have led to new business opportunities beyond television, including movies, home videos, interactive games, toys and merchandise.

Interactive media

Interactive media is one of the fastest growing and most exciting aspects of children's media. This includes the Internet, video games and interactive toys. In addition to the content and business paths, technology is another career course within children's interactive media. There are opportunities for web designers, programmers and web producers.

While the educational benefits of interactive media appear quite promising, there is still much to learn about its impact and how its use should be monitored. With the world at their fingertips, many parents are obviously concerned about letting their children surf on the Internet, but as the Internet has grown, more and more products and services have been introduced to prevent children from stumbling upon adult content. These include filter and blocking software programs like Cyber Patrol, Cyber Sitter, NetNanny and SurfWatch. Content providers like AOL and Yahoo have created "gated play spaces" to guarantee that children will only be exposed to content from reputable sources. Studies have also shown that children don't consume media in a vacuum, but are heavily influenced by parents, older siblings and other authority figures as to what they understand and take away from their media experiences.

Parents are also concerned about the commercialization of the Internet and how easily their children can be influenced by interactive advertising. Content providers are using a variety of methods to identify advertisements within their content, including labels, splash screens and characters to alert children to these paid messages. Of course, depending on the age of the child, no warning or clarification will prove 100 percent effective in preventing commercial messages.

From encouraging violent behavior to promoting a sedentary lifestyle, there have been a variety of concerns about the impact of video games on children as long as the games have existed. Researchers have discovered that playing games is the most common way children from two to eighteen use computers. It's no surprise that they have also found that boys prefer action adventure, sports and violent action games, compared with girls who prefer educational, puzzles, spatial relation and fantasy-adventure games.

Magazines

As with adult titles, kid's magazines have prospered over the last few years, creating and filling new niches that never existed before. Some adult titles like *National Geographic* and *Time* now offer kid's editions. Television brands like Discovery and Nickelodeon have also launched their own magazines targeting kids. To better understand the different career paths available to you in children's magazines, please consult the chapter on magazines in this book.

Merchandising

Merchandising determines the business opportunities for popular children's characters beyond television, film, books and the Internet. It includes toys, licensing, paraphernalia and any other opportunity to expand the brand of a character. Primarily those working in marketing coordinate the various aspects of merchandising – identifying and maintaining strategic partnerships, working with vendors and licensing brands.

Increasingly merchandising has claimed a significant portion of the children's media business, helping to offset the rising production costs of traditional media and the desire of children to experience their favorite character in a variety of different ways. Just two years ago, the worldwide market for children's programs was estimated at $2 billion, but the market for licensed toys alone was worth $27 billion. Five years ago, the majority of the revenue at HIT Entertainment, producer of *Bob the Builder, Barney* and other children's programs, was driven by television. Just two years later, television represented only 20 percent of their revenues, with the remainder being driven by consumer products, home video and stage productions.

INSIGHTS FROM INDUSTRY LEADERS

Deborah Forte

Executive Vice President and President, Scholastic Entertainment

Presented with the daily challenge of bringing Scholastics books to other mediums, Deborah Forte oversees all TV, film, video, interactive and merchandising activities for Scholastic. She has executive-produced more than 300 productions. Television shows produced by Forte have won more than 100 awards. Prior to Scholastic, she headed the specialty sales and marketing group of The Viking Press and Penguin Books.

As a global children's publishing and media company, Scholastic's mission is to instill the love of reading and learning for lifelong pleasure in all children. Some of its most successful titles include *Harry Potter, Clifford the Big Red Dog* and *The Magic School Bus.*

Q: How do you explain the explosion of children's media over the last decade?
A: Finally, children were acknowledged as important viewers. The consolidation of media made broadcasters realize that they had to reach out to children at a younger age. When they saw how successful Nickelodeon was as a 24-hour kids channel, I think many of them felt that just having Saturday morning as the only day part for kids was not a way to help grow their viewership.

When media executives saw all of these specialty channels that were very profitable and drew enough of an audience, they pursued a consolidation strategy. The whole idea was to go from having one demographic to owning a portfolio of channels that would target every demographic.

Q: Historically, the people who typically got involved with children's media had a background in education. Has that changed?
A: I think it needs people who are passionate about kid's programming. People who really care about the audience-and not just about growing their minds, but growing their hearts, stimulating them, making them laugh and making them cry.

You have to have kids as a priority, and it's hard to have kids as a priority when you're programming for adults at the same time. That was my experience before I even got into television. When I was in publishing, I was at a very famous publisher of adult books that also had a children's publishing arm. No one really focused on the kids business because the adult business was the thing that drove the company. I was very happy to come to Scholastic when I did; it was great that everybody here was focused on kids.

Q: What is the most important thing to understand about how children use media today?
A: I think it's just important to understand that it is a part of their life. They are used to interacting with media 24/7, when they want to. Kids, developmentally, like instant gratification. They haven't learned to be patient and wait. They haven't learned to plan. The whole idea that they have to wait until Thursday to see a show when it's Monday seems ludicrous to them. That was the whole idea behind stripping cartoons; you should be able to see it every day if you love it.

Visit Vault at **www.vault.com** for insider company profiles, expert advice, career message boards, expert resume reviews, the Vault Job Board and more.

VAULT CAREER LIBRARY   147

Q: What is the long-term impact on the book market for children?

A: I don't think other media has really started to cannibalize publishing until very recently. The first media format, I think, that has really begun to affect publishing is the DVD. There are so many children who have computers and video gaming systems that play DVDs. It's just ubiquitous. They can make movies and television on DVD a part of their life when they're not watching traditional TV. Particularly with older kids, there's only a certain amount of free time they have. Something's got to give – they have their time in school, they have homework, sports, extracurricular activities, etc. They are faced with the choice to read a book for pleasure, or they can watch a movie or play a video game. Now that DVDs are down to $14.95 and $19.95, I think for the first time there is some cannibalization with books.

Top Kids Books In 2003

Source: Amazon

1. *Harry Potter and the Order of the Phoenix* (Book 5) by J. K. Rowling

2. *Harry Potter and the Order of the Phoenix* (Book 5, Deluxe Edition) by J. K. Rowling

3. *The English Roses* by Madonna

4. *Alice's Adventures in Wonderland: A Pop-up Adaptation* by Lewis Carroll

5. *High Tide in Hawaii (Magic Tree House)* by Mary Pope Osborne

6. *Olivia and the Missing Toy* by Ian Falconer

7. *Diary of a Worm* by Doreen Cronin

8. *Mr. Peabody's Apples* by Madonna

9. *Inkheart* by Cornelia Funke

10. *Loamhedge* (Redwall, Book 16) by Brian Jacques

Understanding How Children Use Media

Impact of television on children

8,000 – Number of TV murders the average child will witness before completing elementary school

100,000 – Number of acts of violence on TV the average child will witness before completing elementary school

300 – Number of studies demonstrating a link between media violence and violent, aggressive, anti-social behavior in children

9% – Portion of parents of children aged two to seventeen who own a TV with a V-chip

39% – Portion of parents of children aged two to seventeen that have never heard of the V-chip

Visit Vault at www.vault.com for insider company profiles, expert advice, career message boards, expert resume reviews, the Vault Job Board and more.

VAULT CAREER LIBRARY   149

79% – Portion of TV shows containing violence that did not receive the appropriate "V" rating

Sources: Congressional Research Service, Kaiser Family Foundation surveys

How children use media

Almost two-thirds (61%) of children now have a television set in their bedrooms; 17% have their own PC.

Based on interviews with 245 children ages eight to seventeen, a 2003 study also shows that 35% of kids have video game systems in their rooms, 14% have their own DVD player, and 9% have Internet access via a PC in their bedrooms.

And the presence of these technologies correlates with significant changes in media behavior:

• 46% do at least half of their TV viewing on their bedroom set.

• 75% report multitasking while watching TV (vs. 65 percent of kids without their own sets).

• 43% have visited a Web site as the result of a TV ad within the past week (vs. 24 percent of kids without their own TVs).

• 50% say they have parental rules for their TV use (vs. 61 percent of kids without their own sets).

The media habits of children who do have Internet access in their own room are revealing:

• 57% say all of their Internet use takes place in their rooms.

• 61% report having parental rules restricting their Web use, compared to 69% of Internet-using kids who do not have own-room Web connections.

Source: Knowledge Networks/SRI Study 2003

Key Players

Networks & programmers

4Kids Entertainment, Inc.

1414 Avenue of the Americas
New York, NY 10019
Phone: 212-758-7666
Web: www.4kidsent.com

ABC Kids

500 S. Buena Vista St.
Burbank, CA 91521-4391
Phone: 818-460-5627
Web: psc.disney.go.com/abcnetworks/toondisney/abckids/index.html

Channel One

1440 Broadway, 17th Fl.
New York, NY 10018
Phone: 212-204-3700
Web: www.channelone.com

DIC Entertainment

4100 W. Alameda Ave., 4th Fl.
Burbank, CA 91505
Phone: 818-955-5400
Web: www.dicentertainment.com

Discovery Kids on NBC

1 Discovery Place
Silver Spring, MD 20910
Phone: 240-662-2000
Web: www.nbc.com/nbc/Discovery_Kids_on_NBC

Disney Channel

3800 W. Alameda Ave.
Burbank, CA 91505
Phone: 818-569-7500
Web: www.disney.go.com/disneychannel/

Visit Vault at **www.vault.com** for insider company profiles, expert advice,
career message boards, expert resume reviews, the Vault Job Board and more.

VAULT CAREER LIBRARY   151

Fox Box

1414 Avenue of the Americas
New York, NY 10019
Phone: 212-758-7666
Web: www.foxbox.tv

Kids WB

4000 Warner Blvd., Bldg. 34R
Burbank, CA 91522
Phone: 818-977-5000
Web: kidswb.warnerbros.com/web/home/home.jsp

Nick Jr. on CBS

1515 Broadway
New York, NY 10036
Phone: 212-258-6000
Web: www.nick.com/all_nick/specials/nick_cbs/

Nickelodeon

1515 Broadway
New York, NY 10036
Phone: 212-258-6000
Web: www.nick.com

Noggin

1515 Broadway
New York, NY 10036
Phone: 212-258-6000
Web: www.noggin.com

PBS Kids

1320 Braddock Place
Alexandria, VA 22314
Phone: 703-739-5000
Web: pbskids.org

Sesame Workshop

1 Lincoln Plaza
New York, NY 10023
Phone: 212-595-3456
Web: www.sesameworkshop.org

The Cartoon Network
190 Marietta St. Northwest
Atlanta, GA 30303
Phone: 404-885-4390
Web: www.cartoonnetwork.com

Publishers

Dorling Kindersley Ltd.
375 Hudson St.
New York, NY 10014
Phone: 212-213-4800
Web: www.dk.com

HarperCollins Children's Books
10 E. 53rd St.
New York, NY 10022
Phone: 212-207-7000
Web: www.harperchildrens.com

Kids Can Press
2250 Military Rd.
Tonawanda, NY 14150
Phone: 866-481-5827
Web: www.kidscanpress.com

Lee & Low
95 Madison Ave., Suite #606
New York, NY 10016
Phone: 212-779-4400
Web: www.leeandlow.com/

Random House
1745 Broadway
New York, NY 10019
Phone: 212-782-9000
Web: www.randomhouse.com

Scholastic
557 Broadway
New York, NY 10012
Phone: 212-343-6100
Web: www.scholastic.com

Visit Vault at **www.vault.com** for insider company profiles, expert advice,
career message boards, expert resume reviews, the Vault Job Board and more.

VAULT CAREER LIBRARY   153

Simon Says
1230 Avenue of the Americas
New York, NY 10020
Phone: 212-698-7000
Web: www.simonsays.com

The Penguin Group
375 Hudson St.
New York, NY 10014
Phone: 212-366-2000
Web: www.penguin.com

Interactive media

www.ajkids.com
Ask Jeeves Kids
5858 Horton St., Ste. 350
Emeryville, CA 94608
Phone: 510-985-7400

Pearson Education
1 Lake St.
Upper Saddle River, NJ 07458
Phone: 201-236-7000
Web: www.juniornet.com

J2 Interactive
16 Harvard St.
Charlestown, MA 02129
Phone: 617-241-7266
Web: www.kaboose.com

Kaboose, Inc.
505 University Ave., Suite 1400
Toronto, ON
M5G 1X3
Phone: 416-593-3000

www.kiddonet.com
420 Lexington Ave., Suite 2531
New York, NY 10170
Phone: 877-543-6835

www.kidscom.com
Circle 1 Network
131 W. Seeboth St.
Milwaukee, WI 53204
Phone: 414-271-5437

Kid's Online (KOL)
America Online
22000 AOL Way
Dulles, VA 20166
Phone: 703-265-1000

Leap Frog
6401 Hollis St., Ste. 150
Emeryville, CA 94608-1090
Phone: 510-420-5000
Web: www.leapfrog.com

www.nationalgeographic.com/kids
National Geographic Society
1145 17th St. NW
Washington, DC 20036-4688
Phone: 202-857-7000

www.nick.com
1515 Broadway
New York, NY 10036
Phone: 212-258-6000

www.toontown.com
3800 W. Alameda Ave.
Burbank, CA 91505
Phone: 818-569-7500

www.yahooligans.com
Yahoo!
701 1st Ave
Sunnyvale, CA 94089
Phone: 408-349-3300

Visit Vault at **www.vault.com** for insider company profiles, expert advice,
career message boards, expert resume reviews, the Vault Job Board and more.

VAULT CAREER LIBRARY   155

www.yucky.com
1 Discovery Place
Silver Spring, MD 20910
Phone: 240-662-2000

Magazines

Cricket
Carus Publishing Company
315 Fifth St.
Peru, IL 61354
Phone: 815-224-5803
Web: www.cricketmag.com

Discovery Girls
1 Discovery Place
Silver Spring, MD 20910
Phone: 240-662-2000
Web: www.discoverygirls.com

Disney Adventures
3800 W. Alameda Ave.
Burbank, CA 91505
Phone: 818-569-7500
Web: disney.go.com/DisneyAdventures/

Highlights
1800 Watermark Dr.
Columbus, OH 43216-0269
Phone: 614-486-0631
Web: www.highlights.com

National Geographic Kids
1145 17th St. NW
Washington, DC 20036-4688
Phone: 202-857-7000
Web: www.nationalgeographic.com/ngkids/index.html

Nickelodeon Magazine
1515 Broadway
New York, NY 10036
Phone: 212-258-6000
Web: www.nick.com/all_nick/nick_mag/index.jhtml

Sports Illustrated For Kids
1271 Avenue of the Americas
New York, NY 10020-1393
Phone: 212-522-1212
Web: www.sikids.com

Time for Kids
Time
1271 Avenue of the Americas
New York, NY 10020-1393
Phone: 212-522-1212
Web: www.timeforkids.com

Weekly Reader
WRC Media
512 7th Ave.
New York, NY 10018
Phone: 212-768-1150
Web: www.weeklyreader.com/kids/

Visit Vault at **www.vault.com** for insider company profiles, expert advice, career message boards, expert resume reviews, the Vault Job Board and more.

VAULT CAREER LIBRARY   157

INNOVATIVE SOLUTIONS

Karen Gruenburg

Executive Vice President, Content, Sesame Workshop

Keeping a Children's Brand Fresh After 35 Years

Challenge

Sesame Street was founded over 35 years ago to address a critical need, that of the educational gap between inner city kids and their suburban counterparts.

There was also an overriding concern that kids deserved something more. The creators believed that kids could grasp bigger concepts, and that they needed to see the world reflected on the television screen. That is why *Sesame Street* was set in an inner city. That's why it had a really diverse cast of people, as well as puppets. The philosophy strove for something bigger and better.

Twenty or thirty years ago, you kept a child watching the program a lot longer. There weren't as many choices. Kids basically lead completely different lives today. When we launched the show there were more kids in the home versus daycare. Kids today expect to have media when, where and how they want it.

Strategy & Solutions

A couple of years ago, during season thirty-three, we completely threw *Sesame Street* upside down and redid the whole format of the show. While still maintaining the philosophy of providing kids with bigger, more and harder concepts to grasp, we started to really look at how to use the real estate we have on air to teach better and to teach deeper. We ended up changing the format of the show. That whole process really caused us to take a hard look at how we deliver content to kids.

It was the largest reinvention. We kept experimenting, and used the hour differently to created new formats within the hour. We looked at the way kids wanted to watch a story. We used to have the street story broken up throughout the hour. We decided to condense it, because we were losing kids' interest, according to our research. We decided to bring back more of our classic Muppets in a more pronounced way. We gave Cookie Monster his own segment. We gave The Count his own segment. We still wanted to play up all the different relationships between the characters, so we put more of that in the street stories and we introduced a new look for *Sesame Street*.

In "Journey to Ernie," a new segment that we collaborated on with our interactive group, we introduced kids to the world in a more pronounced way through Global Grover, in which we used our international film library. We had Grover narrate and introduce kids to the similarities, as well as the differences, of kids around the globe.

We also came to realize we have to look at content holistically. We've always believed that you want to be everywhere a child is, because you need think about the day in the life of a child. You need to be able to provide tools for parents and kids, to entertain them, to delight them, but to ultimately to educate them. We've always been in a variety of different mediums, but now we think a little bit more about the links between some of these mediums and really push the envelope in terms of new technologies.

Each year we pull together a curriculum seminar of outside experts, child development experts and other experts in a variety of fields that touch the lives of kids. We listen to them. We go on a listening tour and they tell us what the hot buttons are, where we should focus.

What we've really started doing since season thirty-three is put an educational philosophy around developing "the thinking child." We develop concepts to help kids think things through, so they get those critical skills that give them confidence to get them ready to learn. It is that thinking process that underscores everything we do on *Sesame Street.* We want kids to figure things out for themselves. We want to develop their innate ability and capture their natural curiosity. It's about sequencing. It's about combining. It's about all of the things that make up the basic kind of skills that get kids to be better learners.

We also decided we wanted to be known as a non-profit company. We were always a non-profit, but we never really discussed that with our consumers or our viewers. The proceeds from the Sesame toys, videos and books all go back into education. That's what keeps Sesame Workshop going and allows us to do it right.

We changed the name of the company from Children's Television Workshop to Sesame Workshop around the same time as well. We knew that Sesame Street was the largest thing that has ever happened to kid's media. Sesame means more than just a television show. To us it meant changing an agenda, the ability to open doors to kids around the world, so we wanted to use that word Sesame in the name of our organization. Workshop is a keyword for our organization, because it is about experimentation, it is about pushing the envelope. Renaming ourselves Sesame Workshop meant something to the organization in terms of the creative spirit and the creative drive. We want to use it to keep engaging kids, but at the same time we wanted to reflect the company, its history and its origin.

Results

We are a very issue oriented media company, but we have done it in a way that is unbelievably entertaining. We have won 97 Emmys. You don't win 97 Emmys unless you are pretty darn creative. It is a very unique blend. Season thirty-three was a whole rethink of what we mean in the world, from *Sesame Street* on air, to how we've organized our company, to the name of our organization, to a desire for a greater awareness around what this organization is all about.

You have to continually reassess. You have to push the envelope, so you stay ahead of the curve. It is that constant self examination that prevents you from being tied to old conventions. That is a big lesson. Sesame Street is very elastic, and it can go in many different ways and in many different places, maintaining the enormous trust with its audience.

It is the conflux of high creative talent, the high educational value and the desire to keep innovating that has made Sesame Street the gold standard for thirty-five years.

Visit Vault at **www.vault.com** for insider company profiles, expert advice, career message boards, expert resume reviews, the Vault Job Board and more.

VAULT CAREER LIBRARY   **159**

The Inside Scoop

Must read

Broadcasting & Cable: Trade magazine providing information about the business of television.
www.broadcastingandcable.com

Cynopsis Kids: Free newsletter dedicated to covering all of children's media.
www.cynopsis.com

MediaWeek: Trade magazine covering the entire media industry.
www.mediaweek.com

Multichannel News: Weekly trade magazine covering the cable industry.
www.multichannelnews.com

Publishers Weekly: Trade magazine dedicated to news and information as it relates to the publishing industry.
www.publishersweekly.com

Variety: Daily trade magazine covering all aspects of the entertainment industry.
www.variety.com

Join the club

American Book Publishers Association
Phone: 212-645-2368
Web: www.ABPAonline.org

American Society of Journalists & Authors
Phone: 212-997-0947
Web: www.asja.org

Association of American Publishers
Phone: 212-255-0200
Web: www.publishers.org

Editorial Freelancers Association
Phone: 212-929-5400
Web: www.the-efa.org

National Academy of Arts & Sciences
Phone: (818)754-2800
Web: www.emmys.org

National Association of Program Executives
Phone: 310-453-4440
Web: www.natpe.org

National Cable Association
Phone: (202) 775-3550
Web: www.ncta.com

Online Publishers Association
Phone: 646-698-8071
Web: www.online-publishers.org

Society of Children's Book Writers & Illustrators
Phone: 323-782-1010
Web: www.scbwi.org

Job leads

Media Bistro
www.mediabistro.com

Publishers Weekly
www.publishersweekly.com

Keep Your Career Moving Forward

Special training

There are no required degrees to land a job in children's media, but the very nature of the content does attract quite a few former educators. As the business has shifted its focus from distribution channels to brands, more and more MBAs are now entering the business as well. As always, internships are highly recommended to gain experience and contacts.

Landing your first job

Be around kids: If you want to work in children's media, you better have something on your resume that demonstrates your ability to work with

Visit Vault at **www.vault.com** for insider company profiles, expert advice, career message boards, expert resume reviews, the Vault Job Board and more.

VAULT CAREER LIBRARY   161

children. Whether or not you are still in college, there are always many opportunities to volunteer to help out underprivileged kids.

The marketing track: Although your dream job may lie on the creative side, more and more marketing opportunities are becoming available. As marketing is on the business side, it generally means more money.

Pay your dues: You won't be producing a hit kid's show or writing a bestseller right off the bat, so don't turn your nose up at those production assistant (PA) jobs. Use the opportunity to see how all the different departments function and maybe you will come across a career path you never thought of before. Also, if you are having a tough time landing a job in kid's media, consider getting a job elsewhere in media, just to start gaining some experience.

Getting your career unstuck

Children's media is all about creativity. If you have an idea, share it. Don't be afraid to speak up when appropriate. Here are a couple of tips when pitching your idea:

1. Be sure it fits in with the overall strategy, mission and direction of the department or company you are working for. If you aren't on the same page as management, your idea will never see the light of day.

2. Develop an argument for your idea. How will it make money? How much will it cost? How will it be produced? Does it fit within the overall strategy? These are all questions a manager must answer to get approval on projects she or he wants to develop, so think like a manager.

3. Share your idea with a colleague you believe you can trust, so she or he can give you some guidance as to whether or not it has any legs. See if there is an opportunity to bring it up in a weekly meeting or some other group setting to establish that it is your idea, so no one else can lay claim to it.

As with other media, making the leap from publishing to television or vice versa can be challenging. If you are unsure as to which path you would like to take, try getting a job at a company that creates content for multiple platforms, like television, film, publishing and the Internet.

Ethnic Media

One of the most significant cultural shifts borne out of the civil rights struggles of the 1960s was a change in America's view of itself as a "melting pot." Since then, the view has shifted towards "multiculturalism," the idea that different ethnicities and nationalities can maintain their unique identity, celebrating their differences within the larger American family.

The release of the 2000 Census figures revealed one of the most dramatic population trends in recent American history: the explosive growth of minority groups, particularly Hispanics, was far outpacing the growth of the white majority. This reality provided even more credence to the growing movement towards greater multiculturalism that characterized the media world during the 1990s.

These demographic changes reflect a significant shift within the established media structure. Media is evolving from serving mass audiences to delivering mass-personalized experiences, helping to promote a greater diversity of voices in American media. The Internet and other digital mediums have dramatically reduced production costs and vastly improved the ability to target specific demographics, providing favorable economic conditions for the establishment of even more ethnic media outlets than ever before.

Current trends

Maintenance of a Strong Identity: It is important to understand the strong desire of many of these rapidly growing ethnic media outlets to maintain their unique identity to best serve their core audience. However, they also desire to reach out to the mainstream audience or "general market" as the white audience is also described, but on their own terms. They would like to invite a wider audience into their distinct cultural community to be appreciated for who they are, but do not want to tailor their content in such a way as to be more acceptable to mainstream tastes.

Green Is Still the Most Important Color: While there is growing excitement about the rainbow of colors filling out the American media landscape, green is still the most important of them all. With an estimated combined buying power of $1.25 trillion among minorities and just 2 percent of all advertising dollars currently spent on ethnic media, there is big money to be made. A 2002 study by New California Media showed that 84 percent

Visit Vault at **www.vault.com** for insider company profiles, expert advice, career message boards, expert resume reviews, the Vault Job Board and more.

VAULT CAREER LIBRARY 163

of the three largest minority groups in California are reached via ethnic media outlets. The most coveted demographic by advertisers remains 18-34 year olds, and it is interesting to note that the average age of Latinos is 24, while the average age of whites is 33.

California: First "Minority Majority" State

Projected Demographics in 2020

Hispanic: 41%
White: 33%
Asian: 18%
Black: 7%

Ultra Niche Ethnic Audiences: The rise of digital cable and the Internet has now made it economically possible to sustain business models that reach audiences only numbering in the tens of thousands. Just five years ago, cable operators would never consider a new channel that couldn't potentially appeal to at least 80 million homes. Many cable operators have now forced newly launched cable networks onto their digital tiers, a premium service for consumers. Some in the industry refer to these premium tiers as the "ethnic ghetto" of cable television, because their target audience must pay an additional fee to view programming they feel should be made available as part of basic cable. The rise of Video On Demand also enables ultra niche ethnic groups that may be too small to sustain a 24/7 linear network to reach out to their communities with on demand programming.

Defining the Urban Demo: The term "urban" used to be a euphemism in the music industry for black radio stations. Ten years ago, there were only six radio stations playing hip hop; today there are well over 150 in the U.S. The term "urban" has taken on a much larger meaning over the last decade, encompassing Hispanics as well as blacks and newly arriving immigrants. The average age of the urban demo is only 26 years old. The urban market now represents some 45 million people with almost $900 billion in buying power. They are more interested in movies and music than television. They are also more inclined to be bicultural than their white counterparts.

Closing the Digital Divide: The Internet is also proving to be a hot opportunity in ethnic media. According to Forrester Research, 68 percent of Asians, 43 percent of Hispanics and 40 percent of blacks access the Internet, vs. 44 percent of whites. In 1996, Community Connect was founded as an umbrella for different online ethnic communities. Today their web properties include AsianAvenue, MiGente, and BlackPlanet, with nearly 8 million members between them.

Snapshot of the Growing Ethnic Diversity in America

- Between 1980 and 2000, the number of people identifying themselves as white fell from 83 percent to 75 percent.

- The number of people speaking their native language at home grew by 48 percent from 1980 to 2000.

- More than 53 percent of the 2,000 participants in the New California Media Study in 2002 said they prefer ethnic media, with Hispanics having the highest level of preference at 59 percent.

- The Editor and Publisher 2003 Yearbook lists 143 weekly ethnic newspapers nationally, covering a wide variety of ethnicities and nationalities.

- In 2002, New York's Independent Press Association counted 200 ethnic newspapers and magazines published in the city, an increase of 33 percent from 1990.

Median Incomes of Ethnic Groups

Asian-Americans: $44,000
Whites: $39,000
Hispanics: $25,000
African-Americans: $24,000

Visit Vault at **www.vault.com** for insider company profiles, expert advice, career message boards, expert resume reviews, the Vault Job Board and more.

VAULT CAREER LIBRARY   165

INSIGHTS FROM INDUSTRY LEADERS

Jorge Gestoso

Broadcast Journalist and Founder of Gestoso Television News

For nearly 20 years, Gestoso has been the face of Spanish-language television news in America. He was an anchor of a nightly news broadcast at Telemundo, and then became the principal anchor on CNN en Español when it launched in 1997. This past May, he left the network to launch his own television news production company, Gestoso Television News (GTN). He envisions producing a wide range of journalistic products, starting with the launching of a new Spanish-language interview program later in 2004.

Q: Despite the explosion of Spanish-language media in the United States over the last decade, do you still think the market might be underserved?
A: I think we are seeing mostly programs that are targeted to the masses. There is still room for improvement in more sophisticated programming aimed at cultural education for Hispanics. We're seeing a lot of standard programming, and there's room for more segmented programming.

Q: What role will the Internet play in continued development of Latino media?
A: We have seen in the general market that the Internet is definitely an integral component of their lives, a complement to the mass media, but not necessarily competition. I would say there has also been a lot of growth among Hispanics, in terms of getting access to computers and to the Internet. It's playing a larger day-to-day role in their lives as a complementary way to get information.

Q: More and more cable networks are being launched, focusing on various ethnicities. Does this trend divide American media along racial lines or does it promote diversity?
A: I think that in some ways there is some risk in promoting diversity. For example, when I catch a plane, and I'm going from South America to Europe and they ask me at the airport, "What's your race?" I say I'm white and that's fine. When I get to the United States, they decide it's not about race, it's about ethnic origin, and suddenly I'm not white anymore. I'm labeled as a Hispanic; labeled as different from other people who are exactly like me.

I don't necessarily see any positives to segmenting people like that, and I don't necessarily agree that you're giving them a larger voice because that voice isn't being heard in the general market. You're putting those people in a corner and they're only going to be able to move within that little corner.

The only thing that I agree with is that it's a way for people to respect their background and their culture. An American whose family came from Ireland three generations ago is considered white, but an American whose family came three generations ago from Mexico is considered Hispanic; I tend to have trouble with that.

Q: What advice do you have for Latino journalists seeking to enter English-speaking or the mainstream media?
A: We have to assume that we are playing on a level field. Given the fact of our background, many times Latinos are considered second- or third-class citizens. You have to assume that you're at least as good as anybody else and you may be even better. Don't enter the profession with any idea that you can only play some sort of secondary role.

Hispanic Media

Spanish-language media has experienced the fastest growth compared with all other ethnic groups and is regarded as one of the hottest marketing and investment opportunities in all of media. The circulation of Spanish-language dailies has more than tripled since 1990. According to the Latino Print Network, ad revenues have grown more than seven times since 1990. The nation's largest and oldest Spanish-language newspapers, *La Opinión* and *El Diario/La Prensa*, recently merged to form Impremedia with an eye on building a national chain of Spanish-language dailies.

In 2001, NBC confirmed the growing importance of Spanish-language media within the larger landscape of mainstream media when it acquired the Spanish-language network Telemundo for $2.7 billion. Since the purchase, it has been estimated that NBC has pumped over $70 million into Telemundo's news gathering operations, as well as leveraging the resources of NBC News.

Powerhouse Univision, the nation's largest Spanish-language media company, recently acquired the Hispanic Broadcasting Company radio group for $3 billion. Some analysts estimate Unvision's overall value at $8 billion at the time of the acquisition.

Almost every major mainstream media outlet has rolled out a Spanish-language version of its brand, from the *Wall Street Journal's* weekly inserts in Hispanic newspapers to *People en Español* to ESPN Desportes. TV Azteca, a Mexican broadcaster, is also slowly grabbing its share of the North American Hispanic market as it begins to build and acquire new television stations in the United States.

Visit Vault at **www.vault.com** for insider company profiles, expert advice, career message boards, expert resume reviews, the Vault Job Board and more.

VAULT CAREER LIBRARY   **167**

Hispanic Media By the Numbers

Population Size: 37 million

*According to Nielsen data from 2003, 65 percent of the Hispanic population is under 35, compared to 45 percent of non-Hispanics.

Demographic Growth:

*In 1980, there were 14.6 million Latinos, representing 6.4 percent of the U.S. population.

*By 2000, there were over 35 million Latinos, representing 12.5 percent of the U.S. population.

*In 2003, Hispanics edged out blacks as the largest minority group in the U.S.

Major Population Centers: New York, Los Angeles, Chicago, Atlanta

Buying Power: $452 billion

*At the time of the purchase of Telemundo by NBC in 2001, NBC estimated that Hispanic buying power would grow to $1 trillion a year by 2010.

Media Fact: According to Arbitron, Latinos are 21 percent more likely than the average American to see a movie within two weeks of its

Key Players: Hispanic

Newspapers

Diario La Estrella (Dallas/Fort Worth)
400 West 7th St.
Fort Worth, TX 76102
Phone: 817-390-7180
Web: www.dfw.com/mld/laestrella

El Diario/La Prensa (New York)
345 Hudson St., 13th Floor
New York, NY 10014
Phone: 212-807-4600
Web: www.eldiariony.com

El Nuevo Herald (Miami)
One Herald Plaza
Miami, FL 33132-1693
Phone: 305-376-3535
Web: www.miami.com/mld/elnuevo

Hoy
330 West 34th St., 17th Floor
New York, NY 10001
Phone: 917-339-0800
Web: www.holahoy.com

La Opinion (Los Angeles)
411 West 5th St.
Los Angeles, CA 90013
Phone: 213-622-8332
Web: www.laopinion.com

Television

CNN en Español
1 CNN Center
Atlanta, GA 30303
Phone: 404-827-1500
Web: www.cnn.com

Hispanic Information and Telecommunications Network
449 Broadway, 3rd Floor
New York, NY 10013
Phone: 212-966-5660
Web: www.hitn.tv

Sí TV
3030 Andrita St. #A
Los Angeles, CA 90065
Phone: 323-256-8900
Web: www.sitv.com

Visit Vault at **www.vault.com** for insider company profiles, expert advice,
career message boards, expert resume reviews, the Vault Job Board and more.

VAULT CAREER LIBRARY   169

TV Azteca
Periférico Sur 4121
Colonia Fuentes del Pedregal
14141 México, D.F., Mexico
Phone: +52-55-3099-1313
Web: www.tvazteca.com.mx

Telemundo
2290 West 8th Ave.
Hialeah, FL 33010
Phone: 305-884-8200
Web: www.telemundo.com

Univision
1999 Avenue of the Stars, Ste. 3050
Los Angeles, CA 90067
Phone: 310-556-7676
Web: www.univision.com

Radio

Entravision Communications
2425 Olympic Blvd., Ste. 6000 West
Santa Monica, CA 90404
Phone: 310-447-3870
Web: www.entravision.com

Spanish Broadcasting
2601 S. Bayshore Dr., PH II
Coconut Grove, FL 33133
Phone: 305-441-6901
Web: www.spanishbroadcasting.com

Univision Radio
3102 Oak Lawn Ave., Ste. 215
Dallas, TX 75219
Phone: 214-525-7700
Web: www.univision.com

Magazines

Latina
1500 Broadway, Suite 700
New York, NY 10036
Phone: 212-642-0200
Web: www.latina.com

People en Español
1271 Avenue of the Americas
New York, NY 10020-1300
Phone: 212-522-7092

Internet

AOL Latin America
6600 N. Andrews Ave., Ste. 400
Fort Lauderdale, FL 33309
Phone: 954-689-3000
Web: www.aola.com

HispanicBusiness.com
425 Pine Ave.
Santa Barbara, CA 93117-3709
Phone: 805-964-4554
Web: www.hispanicbusiness.com

Quepasa Corporation
3 Gateway Center
410 N. 44th St., Ste 450
Phoenix, AZ 85008
Phone: 602-716-0100
Web: www.quepasa.com

Terra Lycos (U.S. Office)
100 5th Ave.
Waltham, MA 02451
Phone: 781-370-2700
Web: www.terralycos.com

Visit Vault at **www.vault.com** for insider company profiles, expert advice,
career message boards, expert resume reviews, the Vault Job Board and more.

VAULT CAREER LIBRARY   171

African-American Media

The first African-American newspaper, *Freedom's Journal*, was founded in 1827 in New York City. Today, the National Newspaper Publishers Association (NNPA), a federation of more than 200 periodicals targeting African-Americans around the country, reaches out to some 15 million readers. The number of black newspapers with an online presence grew from 40 in 2001 to more than 90 by 2003.

In 2000, Viacom announced the acquisition of Black Entertainment Television (BET) for $3 billion. Some in the black community felt they were "sold out" as a result of the acquisition, but BET's corporate chieftains stressed the promise of additional resources to invest in better programming and greater distribution. Since the acquisition, CBS News has provided support for the production of BET News, and specials have been produced in conjunction with CBS Sports. BET.com is the number one Internet portal for African-Americans, and BET has launched a radio network on XM Satellite Radio called BET Uptown.

This year a new African-American network, TV One, was launched, providing lifestyle and entertainment-oriented programming. The Major Broadcasting Network (MBC) changed its name to the Black Family Channel to reflect the new direction of the network. It is currently available in 30 million homes.

In magazines, *Essence, Vibe, Black Enterprise* and *Ebony* remain standard bearers. Publishing impresario Len Burnett is planning to develop a chain of lifestyle magazines built around black neighborhoods. He recently launched the quarterly, *Uptown,* in Harlem, and plans to launch *Bronzeville* in 2005, named after Chicago's South Side neighborhood. As with other magazines, African-American publishers are faced with tight ad budgets, targeting even more focused niche audiences, and the challenge of how to better unlock the potential of their web sites.

African-American Media By the Numbers

Population Size: 36 million

Demographic Growth:

*According to a 2003 Census Report, the black population grew by just 1.5 percent

*1 in 4 African-Americans are between 18 and 34, with an average age of 26.5.

Populations Centers: Atlanta, Washington, D.C., Los Angeles, New York, Chicago, Detroit, Philadelphia, Houston

Buying Power: Approximately $600 billion

*Projected to grow to $965 billion by 2009.

Media Fact: According to Target Market News, in 2003, African-Americans spent $6.2 billion on education versus $2.7 billion on entertainment.

Key Players: African-American

Newspapers

Chicago Defender
2400 S. Michigan Ave., Ste 1
Chicago, IL 60616-2331
Phone: 213-225-2400

The Amsterdam News (New York)
2349 Frederick Douglass Blvd.
New York, NY 10027
Phone: 212-932-7400

The Michigan Citizen (Detroit)
2669 Bagley St.
Detroit, MI 48216-1721
Phone: 313-963-8282

Visit Vault at **www.vault.com** for insider company profiles, expert advice, career message boards, expert resume reviews, the Vault Job Board and more.

VAULT CAREER LIBRARY   173

The Philadelphia New Observer
1520 Locust St., Ste 700
Philadelphia, PA 19102-4406
Phone: 215-545-7500

Television

BET
One BET Plaza
1235 West St., NE
Washington, DC 20018-1211
Phone: 202-608-2000
Web: www.bet.com

TV One
1010 Wayne Ave.
10th Floor
Silver Spring, MD 20910
Phone: 301-755-0400
Web: www.tv-one.tv

Radio

American Urban Radio Networks
960 Penn Ave., Ste 200
Pittsburgh, PA 15222-3811
Phone: 412-456-4000
Web: www.aurnol.com

Radio One
5900 Princess Garden Pkwy., 7th Floor
Lanham, MD 20706
Phone: 301-306-1111
Web: www.radio-one.com

Magazines

Black Enterprise
130 5th Ave., 10th Floor
New York, NY 10011-4399
Phone: 212-242-8000
Web: www.blackenterprise.com

Johnson Publishing
820 S. Michigan Ave.
Chicago, IL 60605
Phone: 312-322-9200
Web: www.ebony.com
Owns: Ebony, JET

Vibe
11100 Santa Monica Ste. 600
Los Angeles, CA 90025-3384
Phone: 310-893-5400
Web: www.vibe.com

Internet

AOL Black Voices
America Online
22000 AOL Way
Dulles, VA 20166
Phone: 703-265-1000
Web: www.blackvoices.com

BlackNews
Diversity City Media
225 West 3rd Street, Suite #203
Long Beach, CA 90802
Phone: 562.209.0616
Web: www.blacknews.com

BlackPlanet
Community Connect
149 5th Ave
New York, NY
Phone: 212-431-4477
Web: www.blackplanet.com

BlackWebPortal
4630 South Kirkman Road, #711
Orlando, FL 32811
Phone: 305.433.7794
Web: www.blackwebportal.com

Visit Vault at **www.vault.com** for insider company profiles, expert advice,
career message boards, expert resume reviews, the Vault Job Board and more.

VAULT CAREER LIBRARY   **175**

Asian-American Media

The greatest challenge facing Asian-American media is the lack of a common language, and in many cases, a common culture. Japanese, Chinese, Indians, Koreans, Thai, Indonesians, Philippines and Vietnamese have all been lumped into one ethnic category by the U.S. Census Bureau. The emergence of digital cable channels, satellite channels and web sites over the last few years now make it possible to build media outlets around specific slices of the Asian-American community, beyond just newspapers and radio broadcasts.

ImaginAsian, a new Asian-American cable channel, is reaching out to all Asians with programming in different Asian languages, as well as English-speaking programs. They also regard Video On Demand as a form of distribution through which they can target different Asian groups with highly specific content.

Asian-American Media By the Numbers

Population Size: 12 million

*The average age of Asian-Americans is 27 years old.

Demographic Growth: Asian-Americans represented 1.5% of the U.S. population in 1980, growing to 3.6% by 2002.

Population Centers: New York, Los Angeles, San Francisco, Seattle, Honolulu

Buying Power: $254 billion

Media Fact: 85% of Asian-Americans still prefer consuming media in their native languages.

Key Players: Asian American

Newspapers

Asahi Shimbun International (Japanese)
757 3rd Ave.
New York, NY 10017
Phone: 212-755-3900
Web: www.asahi.com

Chinese United Journal
83 White St.
New York, NY 10013
Phone: 212-513-1440

India Abroad
43 West 24th St.
New York, NY 10010
Phone: 212-929-1727

Northwest Asian Weekly
412 Maynard Ave. S.
Seattle, WA 98104
Phone: 206-223-5559

The Korea Times
4525 Wilshire Blvd.
Los Angeles, CA 90010
Phone: 323-692-2000
Web: www.koreatimes.com

The World Journal (Chinese-language daily in New York)
141-07 20th Ave.
Whitestone, NY 11357
Phone: 718-746-8889
Web: www.worldjournal.com

Visit Vault at **www.vault.com** for insider company profiles, expert advice,
career message boards, expert resume reviews, the Vault Job Board and more.

VAULT CAREER LIBRARY   177

Television

Bombay Broadcasting
1697 Broadway
New York, NY 10019
Phone: 212-286-9422

Chinese Television System
408 8th Ave.
New York, NY 10001
Phone: 212-947-0851

ImaginAsian TV
19 West 44th St.
9th Floor
New York, NY 10036
Phone: 212-869-4288
Web: www.iatv.tv

Sinovision
15 East 40th St.
New York, NY 10016
Phone: 212-213-6688

TV Asia
76 National Rd.
Edison, NJ 08817
Phone: 732-650-1100
Web: www.tvasiausa.com

Radio

Chinese American Voice
41-25 Kissena Blvd., RM 313
Flushing, NY 11355
Phone: 718-961-6490
Web: www.cavoice.com

EDI KWRM AM 1370
719 N. Sunset Ave.
West Covina, CA 91790
Phone: 626-856-3889
Web: www.am1370-chinese.com

Magazines

AsianWeek
809 Sacramento Street
San Francisco, CA 94108
Phone: (415) 397-0220
Web: www.asianweek.com

Jade Magazine
Village Station
Box 915
New York, NY 10014
Web: www.jademagazine.com

Internet

Sina.com
2988 Campus Dr., Suite 100
San Mateo, CA 94403
Phone: 650-638-9228 x1373

The Inside Scoop

Must read

Cynopsis Multicultural Edition: Free newsletter covering all of ethnic media.
www.cynopsis.com

Diversity Inc.: Newsletter and magazine providing information and resources about diversity.
www.diversityinc.com

ParejaMediaMatch: Bi-weekly newsletter dedicated to Hispanic journalism.
www.parejamediamatch.com

Target Market News: Online resource providing consumer marketing information about the African-American community.
www.targetmarketnews.com

Visit Vault at **www.vault.com** for insider company profiles, expert advice, career message boards, expert resume reviews, the Vault Job Board and more.

VAULT CAREER LIBRARY   179

Join the club

Asian-American Journalists Association
Phone: 415-346-2051
www.aaja.org

National Association of Black Journalists
Phone: 301-445-7100
www.nabj.org

National Association of Hispanic Journalists
Phone: 202-662-7145
www.nahj.org

Native American Journalists Association
Phone: 605-677-5282
www.naja.com

UNITY
Phone: 703-469-2100
www.unityjournalists.org

Job leads

JournalismJobs
www.journalismjobs.com

TVSpy Job Bank
www.tvspy.com

A Word on Diversity

Almost all media companies today have a diversity initiative to ensure all voices are heard within the workplace and the community they serve. Diversity strategies influence decisions at almost every level of a media organization, making sure the employees hired and the content created reflect the needs of their community. Ultimately, diversity helps create more effective relationships between employees and the outside world to better meet the objectives of the organization.

Many editors and news directors have been committed to hiring a diverse group of journalists, but most would agree that there is much room for improvement. Some managers argue that more minorities need to be placed in "gate-keeper" roles, making crucial decisions for the organization that will truly help promote diversity. Many minority journalists opt to work for media outlets in big cities, but working in smaller communities may provide an opportunity to blaze a trail and the chance to bring a fresh perspective to a newsroom that may still offer fairly homogenous coverage.

In a survey from 2000, the Radio and Television News Directors Association (RTNDA) released a study showing 21 percent of all television news employees were minorities and 14 percent of all news directors were minorities. In radio, just 10 percent of the workforce were minorities and only 6 percent of the news directors were minorities.

The American Society of Newspaper Editors published research in 2003 showing that the growth of minority journalists grew by half of one percent in 2002, but still lagged behind the percentage of minorities in the U.S. population, which stood at 31.1 percent. Almost 10 percent of all supervisors in newsrooms were minorities. Asian-Americans saw the largest gain, growing by 152 journalists to 2.62 percent; African-Americans still had the largest representation in newsrooms at 5.33 percent. The number of newspapers with no minority employees dropped from 471 to 373 from the previous year.

Most major newspapers, television stations, magazines and radio stations have diversity officers or managers, overseeing the organization's diversity strategy. When you are applying for a job, in addition to sending your resume to the contact included in the job posting or the human resources department, you should also send a copy of your resume to the diversity officer, so she or he is aware that you are applying for the job. It's another opportunity to make more contacts for your career.

Selected diversity resources

American Society of Newspaper Editors: Diversity
Phone: 703-453-1122
Web: www.asne.org/index.cfm?id=1

CBS News: Diversity Initiative
Phone: 212-975-4321
Web: www.cbsdiversity.com/internship.html

Clear Channel
Phone: 210-822-2828
Web: www.clearchannel.com/Corporate/diversity.aspx

Diversity Best Practices
Phone: 202-466-8209
Web: www.diversitybestpractices.com

Freedom Forum: Newsroom Diversity
Phone: 703-528-0800
Web: www.freedomforum.org/diversity/

Magazine Publishers of America: Diversity
Phone: 212-872-3710
Web: www.magazine.org/diversity

NBC Talent Diversity Initiative
Phone: 212-664-4444
Web: www.nbcjobs.com/NBC_Talent_Diversity_Initiative.html

RTNDA: Diversity
Phone: 202-659-6510
Web: www.rtndf.org/diversity/index.shtml

The New York Times
Phone: 212-556-1234
Web: www.nytco.com/diversity.html

Time Warner: Diversity Initiative
Phone: 212-484-8000
Web: www.timewarner.com/corp/citizenship/diversity

Developing Your Career
In a Digital Media World

CHAPTER 11

Paradigm Shifts

Downsizing, consolidation, outsourcing, synergies, information superhighway, convergence – these are just some of the buzz words that capture the transformation of the American economy from an industrial market to an information-driven one. This shift has revolutionized the media world.

The Internet is changing the very way in which media is produced, distributed and consumed. For decades, the structure of media has been organized around fixed distribution channels like scheduled broadcasts, delivered newspapers or magazine stands. The digital transformation of the media is now untethering both media professionals and consumers from these fixed distribution channels, moving media into a new world organized around intangible relationships and communities.

Mass personalization

The economic model of traditional media is based on a mass market. The more eyeballs a network television show can draw, the more financial success it will enjoy. Digital technologies are now providing marketers and advertisers with the ability to track the effectiveness of their marketing efforts as never before, gathering information about their target customers with startling efficiency. Media is moving from a mass market towards mass personalization, leveraging technology to help maintain more highly personal relationships with individuals within the audience at large. Generating more value from each target customer is increasingly more important than attracting the most customers, some of whom may fall outside of the target demographic.

Community involvement

Costly technology, like printing presses and broadcast transmission towers, created high barriers to entry into the media industry, preventing the average consumer from participating in its creative and production processes. These processes were performed by highly skilled media professionals.

Community involvement has been primarily limited to "letters to the editor," call-in radio shows, and now reality television. Digital technologies are now upsetting this paradigm. The Internet has also lowered the barriers to entry, giving anyone access to a worldwide audience at a very low cost.

The audience at large will play an increasingly important role in media going forward. There is value to incorporating content generated by the consumer into the established professional media, as people who are given the opportunity to contribute to a community feel a greater commitment to it. Increasingly, media communities will be organized around lifestyles, passions or causes.

Here's a closer look at each community type:

Lifestyle: A community based on a shared way of life relating to geography, ethnicity, sexual orientation, religion or culture.

Passion: A community based around a specific interest that provides pleasure or enjoyment, activities like hobbies, work or sports.

Social Cause: A community based around a specific social or political issue. These communities can be borne out of health crises, political concerns or social changes.

Of course, there are obvious overlaps. There is the potential for a social cause to turn into a passion and then into a lifestyle. Some communities will elicit greater levels of individual commitment than others; some will suffer short life spans. The role of media professionals will be to serve as a "guide" to these communities – to help them manage and develop the content they create.

Impact on your career

How will the transition towards a media world based on relationships and communities impact your career? It's important to remember that for a long time to come, there will still be core disciplines like producing, editing, accounting and web designing.

However, non-traditional skills and less tangible qualities are increasingly emphasized. In a recent executive survey conducted by Fordham Business School, digital media executives at the top 25 media companies expressed their desire for candidates who are creative, entrepreneurial, have an understanding of technology and an appreciation of basic business skills. Of course, this is a broad brush stroke that covers many different types of positions, but it demonstrates the increasing convergence of the creative, business and technology sides of media.

No matter where you stand on the proverbial corporate ladder, your career options are changing.

Entry level – don't wait for a job to gain experience

The greatest opportunity in regard to digital technology is that it has removed almost all of the cost involved with producing and distributing media. Just 10 years ago, if you wanted to pursue a career in media, you had almost no choice but to land an entry-level job at a television station, magazine or newspaper. That is no longer true for two reasons:

1. Just as digital technologies are creating new opportunities, they are also taking them away. Software-based business and production applications are reducing the need for an administrative staff.

2. If you want to pursue a career as a writer, you can start gaining experience right now by starting your own weblog. If you are interested in producing video media, you can buy your own digital video camera and editing software (while still a few thousand dollars, it is a fraction of the cost of broadcast equipment, and the price is coming down every day). Most importantly of all, the Internet allows you to distribute your content.

Mid-level – a bridge to the future

Media professionals with 10 to 20 years of experience are a bridge between the past and the future. The essence of media is entertaining and informing through storytelling, but traditional forms of distribution are losing their economic potency.

There are many media professionals in their mid-career who feel frustrated or uncertain about their future career path. This is primarily due to the fact that they will be working in two parallel worlds as the growth of the digital world accelerates and traditional media forms decline.

Corporate structures in media are also starting to become "flatter," moving, as other industries have, from vertical hierarchies to horizontal ones. Because of this, traditional promotions into senior management are less assured.

As clichéd as it sounds, think outside the box. Increasingly, senior executives are less certain about leading their organization in the unfolding digital landscape. Demonstrate leadership. Present new opportunities, especially if

Visit Vault at **www.vault.com** for insider company profiles, expert advice, career message boards, expert resume reviews, the Vault Job Board and more.

VAULT CAREER LIBRARY   **185**

you can show how they will make money. Don't simply focus on cutting costs, focus on creating growth as well. Keep thinking, "create community using technology."

Senior level – leadership for creativity

Senior executives still hold most of the cards within the media industry right now. Many of them passionately embraced Internet opportunities in the late 1990s and were the primary drivers of its growth. Unfortunately, many of them also got burned when everything went bust and have shied away from the Internet ever since. The dot-com collapse wasn't about traditional media winning and the Internet losing, it was about unsound business practices. Some executives are now dipping their toe back into the digital pool. Some sectors as a whole, like cable and satellite, are aggressively pursuing a unified digital strategy.

While they say, "it's hard to teach an old dog new tricks," if you want to continue to lead a media organization, you are never too old to learn new things. Senior executives, who have spent 25 years or more in the business, should be promoting a creative environment among their staff, who will help unlock the full potential of digital technologies. Involving younger members of one's staff has never been more crucial, as it is their generation's media habits that foretell the future structure of the media world.

Preparedness of Each Medium for the Digital World

During the late 1990s, most media companies were swept up in the "get rich quick" schemes that characterized the first wave of the Internet. Some, like Primedia, really took it on the chin. Others, who were heavily criticized during the run-up of the stock market for their risk-averse strategies (like Viacom), ended up big winners by keeping their financial losses to a minimum. Many traditional media companies set up separate divisions in hopes of spinning them off into new companies. With the collapse of the dot-coms, traditional media withdrew their newly established interactive enterprises into the traditional corporate structure and licked their financial wounds. After four years to think and strategize, just how prepared is each sector to take on the "second wave of the Internet," and the new desire for on-demand media?

Television

Cable and satellite television are locked in a dog fight, competing for each and every customer. Satellite growth is booming, coming at the expense of cable, which is experiencing flat growth. Satellite is offering lower prices, a digital picture and Personal Video Recorders. After investing billions over the last decade to upgrade to digital, cable has transformed itself from one product to offering a "triple play" of services, including video services, high-speed Internet access and Internet telephony to its customers as a package for one price.

Broadcast television is probably the most reluctant segment of television to pursue new digital opportunities. Pulling in over $90 billion at the upfront in May 2004, broadcast is anything but a dying business, but it's not preparing itself for the future. It regards its ability to command the largest mass audiences as its single greatest competitive advantage, at a time when consumer media behavior is moving into an on-demand world based on mass personalization. "One size fits all" may have been the wining formula for network television for the last 50 years, but consumers increasingly want to be catered to. Personal Video Recorders threaten the 30-second spot, consumers have more media choices with every passing day and television will increasingly become as "searchable" as the Internet, undercutting the networks' dominance.

In television news, the network evening newscasts still dominate. The perennial third place, *CBS Evening News*, pulls in an average of 8 million viewers each night, while the top-rated show in cable news, *The O'Reilly Factor*, garners just 2 million. However, people can now get their news anytime, anywhere and virtually any way that is most convenient for them. ABC News has caught onto this behavioral shift, rolling out a new service called *ABC Now*, in which ABC News content is delivered on-demand via digital cable, broadband and cell phones, in addition to through traditional broadcasts. It is a model to be watched closely.

Local broadcasters have been even more reluctant to embrace the Internet and digital opportunities. Most have neglected their web sites and are still purely focused on the short-term success of their broadcasts. In an ever-cluttered media landscape, the single best competitive opportunity for local broadcasters is just that, being local. Local broadcasters are well positioned to transform themselves into local media companies, driving value and growth by laser-focus on the local communities they serve. Their web sites will prove to be the foundation of their overall operations, eventually becoming the core of the local community media.

Visit Vault at **www.vault.com** for insider company profiles, expert advice, career message boards, expert resume reviews, the Vault Job Board and more.

VAULT CAREER LIBRARY   **187**

Radio

Last year, the FCC's proposal to further loosen media ownership rules was thwarted by the public's outcry against more consolidation. The trend of consolidation has been more acute in radio than in other media sectors. Almost overnight, Clear Channel Communications grew from a radio group of 100 stations in 1995 to become the largest radio owner in the United States, with over 1,200 radio stations today.

Those in favor of consolidation argue that it has helped to bring higher quality programming to smaller markets, while opponents say it is squashing the voices of thousands of local communities across the U.S. For many small communities, radio is one of the few outlets for local news. It is still relatively inexpensive to produce compared with other media and can broadcast over large, sparsely populated areas.

Consolidation and the current indecency debate are driving more and more radio stations to spring up online, providing service to people all over the world.

Satellite radio services like XM Satellite Radio are also providing an alternative to radio stations that get bumped off the air or don't make the cut. Howard Stern made history in 2004, signing a $500 million deal to join XM Satellite Radio. Independent radio stations, public stations and smaller station groups are now taking the lead in providing more local content, and many in radio believe that local content is the future of free, over-the-air radio.

Magazines

Magazines can be described as the "passion" medium in a media world based on communities and relationships. Just as the Internet is influencing other mediums to become more interactive by creating a two-way path with the community, the magazine's strength has been its ability to build content around specific interests. Magazine giants like Meredith Publishing constantly monitor changing tastes and trends, looking for emerging interests around which to build a new magazine.

Magazines have yet been unable to translate the passion that suffuses their newsstand titles onto the Internet. Their web sites are mostly literal translations of their print product. Moving forward, content will no longer be presented as it is in magazines, but will increasingly be organized in databases, so individuals can access the information in a way that is most meaningful to them. Magazines have been ingenious in recognizing trends, but to succeed online they must learn how to become an engaging interactive resource.

Newspapers

Like magazines, many newspaper web sites are literal copies of their print versions. However, newspaper web sites are probably the most advanced at archiving content and organizing it into rudimentary databases. Some sites are getting better at "packaging" archived content, making it more useful for consumers. At this point in time, the Internet has been a fairly successful text medium, but it will increasingly become a video medium as well. Newspaper folks also have the advantage of thinking in text, as opposed to those working in television and radio.

It can also be argued that newspapers have been the most aggressive in learning how to turn their web properties into profitable businesses. The economic threat has been more acute for newspapers than it has for magazines or broadcasters so far. It's no secret that web behemoths like Monster and Google have taken a chunk of local ad dollars away from newspapers. However, newspapers are fighting back, forming consortiums like Career Builder for online recruitment, as well as improving integration of their print product with their web sites. *The Wall Street Journal* claims to have over 600,000 paying online subscribers. *The New York Times* has gained recognition for its creative and aggressive advertising efforts as well.

Managing Change

The most difficult challenge for most human beings is to accept change. Just as we get settled into the latest formula for creating media, it changes.

Change makes our future less clear and increases our desire to hold onto the comfort of our existing knowledge. It's always harder to build a new frame of reference, but constant change is now part of the institutional process of media.

Whether you are getting started in the media business or starting to get frustrated with it, here are a few thoughts on how to manage change:

Listen: The most important aspect of communication and probably the least practiced. Be open to new ideas. Let others be heard. You never know where new solutions or ideas may come from.

Learn: Always be willing to try new things. With new technologies being introduced as fast as they are, you really have no choice if you want a career in media today. If you aren't learning new skills, there is someone else willing to do so. Guess who will get the job or be promoted?

Passion: If you don't love media, definitely consider another career. Also, avoid focusing exclusively on a particular medium like television, radio, newspapers or the Internet. Instead, focus on a particular content area that you care deeply about, like health, sports or finance. In the years to come, media professionals will be defined by the content they create, not by the distribution channel that delivers their content.

Take Responsibility: It always seems easier to blame someone else for your frustration or problems. Don't give all your power away to someone else and wait for them to solve your problems. Confront them and initiate a dialogue.

Moment for Yourself: With all the demands placed on us today, it's important to take a break. Taking just five minutes to meditate or to go for a quick walk during your workday will reduce your stress, keep you sharper and make you less frustrated.

Focus on Today: We always seem to be focused on the future, something that hasn't even happened yet and something we have no control over. Just worry about what is right in front of you and give it your full attention.

Enduring Career Goals: Think of your career goals as a life mission statement. If you create restrictive short-term goals like working for a certain company, achieving a certain salary or attaining a specific title, you may be setting yourself up for disappointment. Create goals that are consistent, yet enduring, no matter where you work or in what area of media you find yourself.

Just Change: If you are miserable or extremely unhappy, just change. Break your cycle, do something different. Do something you normally wouldn't.

The introduction of new technologies has greatly accelerated over the last decade and shows no sign of slowing down. As much as it is making our lives more efficient, it's also putting new demands on us.

In the media world, new technologies have created completely new revenue streams, businesses and industries. They can also be blamed for the loss of jobs in traditional media. New technologies are liberating creativity, vastly reducing the cost of mistakes. At the same time, they are eating away at established formulas, methods and structures, leaving the media business less focused and unclear. There is now a greater diversity of voices in the overall media process, yet media consolidation threatens to showcase only the most vocal. Media is converging and diverging all at the same time. One constant will remain, however: people will always want great stories, whether for entertainment or information, no matter what the latest delivery mechanism happens to be.

Good luck with all your future endeavors!

Visit Vault at **www.vault.com** for insider company profiles, expert advice,
career message boards, expert resume reviews, the Vault Job Board and more.

VAULT CAREER LIBRARY   191

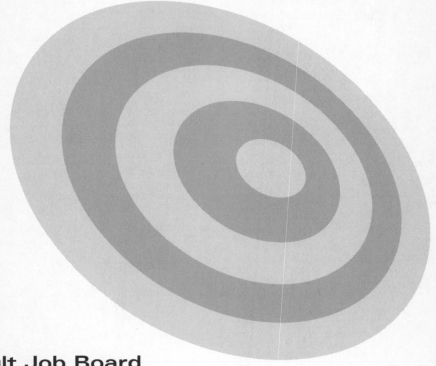

About the Author

Stephen Warley

Currently the General Manager of TVSpy.com, a subsidiary of Vault, Inc. He oversees all content production, marketing and revenue development for TVSpy. He is also the Editor-in-Chief of Next Generation TV, a newsletter dedicated to emerging opportunities in television and video media. He recently completed his MBA in media management and finance at Fordham Business School. As part of his MBA, he conducted an executive survey of the digital media strategies of the top 25 media companies, including interviews with Eddy Hartenstein, Vice Chairman of DIRECTV, Dennis FitzSimons, CEO of Tribune and Martin Nisenholtz, CEO of New York Times Digital. Prior to TVSpy, he served as project manager at ThirdAge Media and as a segment producer at CNBC. He has also produced and provided production support for various CBS broadcasts including *CBS News Sunday Morning, The Early Show*, CBS Sports' coverage of the XVIII Winter Olympic Games in Nagano, Japan, as well as for special broadcasts, *America Under Attack, America Fights Back* and *Death of a Princess*. He graduated magna cum laude with a BA in History from Providence College in 1996.

Visit Vault at **www.vault.com** for insider company profiles, expert advice, career message boards, expert resume reviews, the Vault Job Board and more.

VAULT CAREER LIBRARY 193

Wondering what it's like to work at a specific television company?

Read what **EMPLOYEES** have to say about:

- Workplace culture
- Compensation
- Hours
- Diversity
- Hiring process

Read employer surveys on THOUSANDS of top employers in telvision.